Date Due

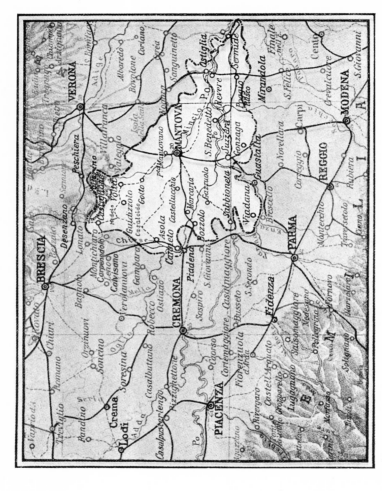

MAP 1. *From the frontispiece of Mantova, issued by the Camera di Commercio e Industria di Mantova for the Ente Nazionale Industrie Turistiche, Rome, 1927.*

IN QUEST OF
VIRGIL'S BIRTHPLACE

LONDON : HUMPHREY MILFORD

OXFORD UNIVERSITY PRESS

IN QUEST OF
VIRGIL'S BIRTHPLACE

By

Edward Kennard Rand

Edward Kennard Rand

CAMBRIDGE
HARVARD UNIVERSITY PRESS
1930

2023

TO

MY FELLOW–VOYAGER

PREFACE

WHERE was Virgil born? The question assumes a new importance as the world turns devoutly to the celebration of his two-thousandth birthday. The ancient tradition that his birthplace was the little town of Pietole, three Roman miles or so to the south of Mantua, has been rudely shaken of late by Professor Conway, who locates the spot thirty miles to the northwest at Calvisano or Carpenedolo. I regret unspeakably to enter into controversy with so dear a friend of mine and so devoted an interpreter of Virgil, but he will forgive me if I speak out my convictions with his own directness. The reader should not swallow my arguments whole, or my statement of those of Conway, but turn first of all to his admirable essay on the subject in his *Harvard Lectures on the Vergilian Age*, published by the Harvard University Press in 1928. My own exposition, sketchy and incidental as the plan of the little book requires, should be supplemented by Bruno Nardi's work, *La Giovinezza di Virgilio*, Mantua, 1927, with an appendix entitled "Il Paese Natio di Virgilio." I had not read this work at the time of our excursion and was delighted to find in it my own deductions with regard to Virgil's birthplace set forth with more system and completeness; certain differences in details do not mar the general uniformity of our points of view. Professor Nardi's volume, small in

PREFACE

compass and rich in contents, has been translated by Mrs. Rand, and in its English form will shortly be issued by the Harvard University Press. I am grateful to the Press for preparing with extra speed these little presents for Virgil's birthday.

E. K. RAND

HARVARD UNIVERSITY
March 1, 1930

CONTENTS

LIST OF ILLUSTRATIONS AND MAPS

LIST OF ILLUSTRATIONS

LIST OF ILLUSTRATIONS

LIST OF ILLUSTRATIONS

LIST OF ILLUSTRATIONS

IN QUEST OF
VIRGIL'S BIRTHPLACE

MANTUA ME GENUIT

From the frontispiece of Notizie Storiche della Città e dello Stato di Mantova. Scritte da
Giovanni Visi Mantovano. Dall' anno di Cristo 990 sino all'anno 1183, *Mantova, 1782.*

IN QUEST OF
VIRGIL'S BIRTHPLACE

Quell' ombra gentil per cui si noma
Pietola piu che villa Mantovana.[1]

I. THE PROBLEM

TO DANTE and the men of his time, the tiny town of Pietola, or Pietole as it is called today, could pride itself on a higher title than that of a suburb of Mantua, since it was there that the poet Virgil was born. The daughter was fairer than the mother fair — men thought of it not as *villa Mantovana* but as *il luogo natale di Virgilio.* Tradition had identified it with the hamlet of Andes cited as Virgil's birthplace by various ancient scholars who wrote of his life.[2] In 1881, the citizens of Mantua — and all the world — commemorated worthily the nineteenth centenary of Virgil's death. For this occasion Tennyson wrote his noble ode, and Carducci delivered his no less noble oration in honor of the poet. Three years later, the poet's countrymen erected at Pietole the admirable statue that the traveler sees today. It seems at home in the little park of hemlocks, chestnuts and poplars, alive with singing birds

Full of some sweet unwonted joy.[3]

At the rear there is a view of vines wedded to their supporting trees in the ancient way. On the base of the statue are inscribed, in front,

[3]

the verses of Dante just quoted. On the left side is a line from the
Aeneid:

And now thy glory guards thine own abode.[4]

On the right stands a line from the passage — taken by Carducci as
a text for his speech — in which Virgil prophesies the erection of a
temple, an epic temple reared in honor of Augustus and all Rome,
but set by the slow-winding streams and reed-fringed banks of the
poet's native Mincio.[5] In the rear are the words

PIETOLE · ERESSE · IL · XX · SETTEMBRE 1884.

The statue expresses the gratitude of posterity, and thus Pietole
seems sanctioned for all time as the spot of the poet's birth.

But hoary error, however beautified by ages of veneration, must
yield to the assault of modern research. One of England's most
eminent scholars, for many stimulating essays *optime de Vergilio
meritus*, has recently declared that the ancient tradition cannot
stand and that the handsome column erected to Virgil should be ex-
ploded.[6] Professor Conway is professionally and temperamentally
no iconoclast. He has been led to his conclusion by weighty arguments; if they are sound, Virgil himself would swing the first pick at
his monument at Pietole. We begin with the explicit statement in
the life of Virgil attributed to Marcus Valerius Probus, a noted
scholar of the first century A.D., that the hamlet of Andes was 30
miles distant from the city of Mantua;[7] these are Roman miles,
equivalent to about 28 English miles or 45 kilometres. That might
seem somewhat remote for a suburb of Mantua, had not Mommsen shown that important Roman townships could cover an even

[4]

larger area than 30 miles. Now exactly 30 miles from Mantua, in the northwest direction towards Brescia, lies Calvisano, the very spot where an inscription was found recording the payment of a vow by a certain Vergilia. Thousands of ancient inscriptions have been found in North Italy; but among them no more than nine contain the name Vergilius or Vergilia. Four of these are from townships remote from Mantua; three are from Verona; one is from Pietole, but it exists only in a copy which Mommsen branded as a forgery.[8] Moreover, at the village of Casalpoglio, only 7½ English miles from Calvisano, an inscription was discovered on a tomb erected by Publius Magius for himself and his wife. Here we have the maternal side of Virgil's family; for his mother was Magia Polla.

To this important inscriptional evidence Professor Conway further contributes a novel and appreciative study of the scenery pictured in Virgil's *Eclogues*. Certain critics have pointed out, with no little scorn, that the poet's pictures bear no relation to the actual sites that he professes to describe. How can anybody, for instance, see evening shadows lengthen from mountain-sides in the marshland of Mantua and little Pietole? Some, therefore, have accused Virgil of glaring incongruities and shameless pilferings from Theocritus. Professor Conway comes to the poet's rescue with a neat distinction. In the even-numbered eclogues, 2, 4, 6, 8 and 10, the scenery is indeed idealized; the poet constructs it imaginatively. In the odd-numbered eclogues, however, particularly in the first and the ninth, the scenery is intentionally local. This principle becomes evident if we transfer the site of the farm to the vicinity of Calvisano. From there one can usually see the foot-hills of the Brescian Alps, and, on clear days, the snowy peaks behind them. Moreover, at Carpenedolo, $5\frac{1}{4}$ miles eastward, there is a prominent ridge which is the first height of land encountered by the traveller proceeding north-west from Mantua and which seems exactly to mark the spot where, in the poet's language, the hills "melt into the plain." The farm ran from that point "down to the water and the old beech-trees." [9] It extended, therefore, from some point of the Carpenedolo ridge down to the river Chiese.[10]

Such is Professor Conway's triple argument, set forth with learning and a charming plausibility. It is of some consequence to the citizens of Mantua if he is right. It likewise behooves the thousands and tens of thousands who are celebrating Virgil's bimillenary this year to begin with a general understanding, if such can be reached, as to just where the poet was born. Ultimately, perhaps, it does not matter much. He was born in the township of Mantua and encompassed in his mind the Roman Empire and the world to come. However, no detail is too trifling if the study of it can throw any light on the poet's art, and the search for something tiny may lead one through pleasant paths. Prompted by inquisitiveness, a rankling doubt as to my friend Conway's conclusions, and a stubborn regard for old traditions of any sort, I set out with my wife and fellow-observer on a pleasant pilgrimage, to which I now invite the reader, in quest of Virgil's birthplace. Our pace is leisurely; we shall stop for anything that attracts us on the way.

II. MILAN TO CREMONA

We started from Milan, where Virgil passed what we should call his undergraduate days, having spent his early years at Cremona. It was there that he assumed the *toga virilis* in his fifteenth year.[11] It was his "coming out"; for, in the masculine age of ancient Rome,

FIGURE 1. THE AMBROSIAN LIBRARY

young gentlemen, not young ladies, were thus introduced to the society of their elders. Perhaps he began his education at Andes — wherever that was — though he evidently did not stay there long. Surely he did not long inhabit the precise place of his birth, if one may believe, with his ancient biographer Donatus, that his mother Magia was delivered of her boy in a ditch.[12] In going from Milan to Cremona and from Cremona to Mantua, we were reversing the order of young Virgil's itinerary when he set forth from home. And we were traversing ground that he must have known well.

We began our homage to Virgil with a visit to the Ambrosian Library, to see with our own eyes the copy of the poet's works once owned by Petrarch, a manuscript of the fourteenth century, written in a sumptuous script with copious comments in the margins; these were supplemented by still further observations in the poet's own hand. Some years ago, I had the pleasure of meeting in the Ambrosian Library its courteous prefect, Monsignor Ratti, now his Holiness Pope Pius XI. In an alcove in one of the galleries they have set his statue, the base of which bears the following inscription:

ACHILLIS · RATTI · HOC
FUIT · CVBICVLVM · AB · ANNO
MDCCCCVII · AD · MDCCCCXI
PRIVSQVAM · IS · BYBLIOTHECAE
VATICANAE · PRAEFICERETUR
ARCHIEPISCOPVS · DEINCEPS
MEDIOLANENSES · REGERET
PIVS · XI · PONTIFEX · MAXIMVS
EXSISTERET
HVIVS · LOCI · INTRA · FINEM
QVISQVIS · INGREDERIS
ARTIBVS · INGENVIS · VT
VTARIS · TANTI · ADMONERE
ET · HOMINIS · ET · NOMINIS
ADMONERE · CVM · NVMINE
ET · OMINE
POSITVM · AN · MDCCCCXXVI

This injunction we took indeed as a good omen, coming from the cubicle of the former librarian of the Ambrosian, and a good sanction for humanistic adventures, such as were then, and are now, dear to him.

We returned to our Hotel Manin, for a final repast in its dining-garden, which has something of the flavor of the gardens of old.

FIGURE 2. GARDEN OF THE HOTEL MANIN, MILAN

We were to proceed in state, thanks to the coöperation of that useful friend of foreigners, Tommaso Cook, who had instructed an admirable chauffeur, Pietro Ferrari, of the Garage Diana, Milan, to be our guide, philosopher and friend. Some poet must have christened that garage. We appropriated the name for the car, which, like the goddess and her nymph Camilla can

Scour the plain,
Fly o'er th' unbending corn, and skim along the main —

and also move at a leisurely pace or loiter by the way. Pietro knew the country well, and aware of our purpose was big with information. He spoke English, though he was glad, when the waters of conversation became deep, to plunge into his native idiom. But when

FIGURE 3. PIETRO AND DIANA

we approached a hotel, he would brush the rabble from before us and in loud tones assume the English language like a royal robe.

On the way out of the city, we pass a great aviation field, which possibly in memory of one who told the story of Daedalus is called the Piazza Ovidio. Italy of today looks back to Classical antiquity, which some moderns of other countries find dead, as to the living soil from which it has drawn strength through all the ages. Ovid and Virgil are not text-books, but Italian poets, present as are all the mighty dead, Dante and Petrarch and Leopardi, in the affections of living men. Even Italian architecture still adheres to ancient models. An unpretentious house that we pass before long recalls some little villa of the Renaissance. Give Nature a decade and the pas-

FIGURE 4. MODERN HOUSE AT PANDINO

ser-by will think it veritably old. It is only a specimen of countless structures that we saw. Contrast them with the ugly novelties that clutter an American, or an English, or even a French landscape! Florence will always remain a city of Dante's time and of the Renaissance, and none the less North Italy, despite its progressiveness, holds loyally to the ancient way. And if we turn back from the Renaissance and the Middle Ages to the houses of Roman Ostia, as recently restored,[13] we discover the lineage of the palazzi.

We are out among the green fields. Crops of Gran Turco corn are frequent. It is used for pollenta, not eaten on the cob in American

FIGURE 5. HOUSE AT OSTIA (restored)

style, though three quarters of the amount required for Italian needs comes from America. Pietro is instructed in the proper method of preparing and eating corn and proceeds with enthusiasm to abstract a few ears from a field near the road. Caught in the act by the tiny daughter of the proprietor, he makes a graceful apology — and anyway the corn was too far developed to be toothsome. The leaves of

FIGURE 6. CANALE MUZZA

the corn, which are unduly fattening, are not given to cattle for fodder, but supply them with their beds.

Along the road we notice canals with bordering hedges, often formed of a stiffish willow called *gaba*, — so said Pietro, — the lower branches of which are cut in the third year and used for fire-wood. The canals are employed for irrigation. Near Milan, they come from the Lago Maggiore; at a farther point in our journey the Adda is tapped. Sometimes they attain impressive proportions, and might well seem to the uninformed traveller natural streams. Such is Canale Muzza near the village of Paullo.

Not only the *gaba* but other trees border the banks, particularly planes and mulberries. Their function, as in most human activities,

FIGURE 7. CANAL AND ITS LOCK

shows a proper combination of altruism and egoism; their roots at once prevent the banks from caving in and draw their own sustenance from the stream. The water of a canal is diverted from its bed by blocking, or locking, the passage with a wooden key. This key, placed just below a transverse canal, forces into this the stream running parallel with the road. The flow is then received by numerous trenches running out from the transverse canal, and the field is flooded. The water stays generally for two days, and then returns to the canal or is shifted to some other field. In this way a rich soil is developed in which grass, like the Blue Grass of Kentucky, is never sown. It springs of itself, grows quickly and is cut for hay four times in the year. Old Varro's story about the pole that, left out in the grass of Rosea at night, was over-grown next morning contains an element

FIGURE 8. A FLOODED FIELD

of truth.[14] And Virgil knew of Mantuan grass that cropped by cattle in the long day grew back during the short but dewy night.[15] With such flooded fields, of which we saw a specimen in the village of Palazzo Pignano, and with the constant Sun, who, as the poet has it in verses of sizzling sibilants,

> Parches the thirsty throats of hollow streams
> And turns their waters into steaming mud,[16]

even the cultivation of rice is profitable. It is no easy game, for the lush grass must be frequently extracted. But *labor (et pecunia) omnia vincit*; girls may be found to weed the crop and cook their feet in the steaming muck for twenty-five lire (a dollar and a quarter) a day.

The fields are further enriched with manure, of which we see well-apportioned heaps from time to time, such as the horny-handed farmer of the *Georgics*, least sentimental of poetical rustics, worked

FIGURE 9. A COUNTRY ICE–HOUSE

lustily into the ground.[17] There are flourishing gardens, with some ancient and some modern vegetables, like the tomato. Poplars and planes, willows and mulberries fly past us. Pines and cypresses are rare, but they can be grown at will and now and then adorn some wealthy man's estate. Beeches do not appear, but Pietro has seen them north of Milan. Fruit-trees are not so plentiful as the mulberry, grown to feed the worms that spin the profitable silk. That is why the mulberry, in this part of the country, replaces the elm as a support for the vine. Ice is stored under picturesque cones of straw.

It is not squandered in beverages — except at Americanized bars — but is useful in the making of butter and cheese. We stop to examine the *Latteria moderna* of Alberto Lang, whose name suggests an Alpine origin and whose electrified vats would have opened Virgil's eyes wide with admiration.

FIGURE 10. MODERN CHEESE-VATS

More modernity confronts us as we squeeze past a gang of work-men bestowing a coat of tar on the road — American tar it is, im-ported by order of Mussolini. But now a pair of old-fashioned oxen draw a shapely load of hay; in the field an ox and a horse yoked to-gether are ploughing the rich tilth; and there is sun-burned The-stylis doing her share of the reaping. No idlers are in sight — except two boys wading in the canal — but toilers can take their labor com-fortably. A man with a load of leaves on his back treadles by us on his bicycle; his head is sheltered by an umbrella of which the handle is fastened to his jacket; his mouth holds a cigar. Now a rustic sleeping in his loaded cart is drawn by his wakeful horse: the horse's brow is shaded by a leafy branch, and a larger one protects his master. Boughs are skilfully wrought into road-side shelters, interlaced with

FIGURE 11. A WAY-SIDE SHELTER

branches of trees, propped with poles, and roofed with leaves and thatch. Such retreats replace the pastoral grottoes in a flat country. They can harbor a whole family at noon-time.

As we glide on our way, I am tempted by these leafy shelters to reinterpret a passage in Virgil. Willows and the lowly broom, he says, give either

To cattle leaves or to the shepherds shade,
For sown fields hedges and for honey food.[18]

[18]

Whether both the broom and the willow serve all these needs is a question. Willows, whether of the stiff kind (*gaba*) or the pliant (*salice*), are often used today to bound a cultivated field, and the broom may well serve the same purpose. Willow-leaves are stripped to make bedding for cattle, but there are few leaves on the broom. Bees feed on the flowers of both, and shepherds may repose in their shade — that is, of the willows; possibly the broom is also meant, for it grows to a height of eight feet.[19] In that case, however, the poet might have used some other epithet than *humilis*.[20] Now brooms as well as reeds would come in handy for making the roof of such shelters as those that we saw in abundance along the way. Perhaps, then, the ancient Roman made them too, finding broom as well as willow useful in the process. Ah yes, there is where Thestylis made the reapers their noon-day salad, garlic not forgotten.

We have crossed the Adda, and left Crema behind, with its lovely campanile and church, within which, far from the noisy world, priests are intoning Vespers. We pass Soresina, Casalmorano, Casabuttano. Here comes a pretty girl on a bicycle, her parasol held daintily over her head. There are some youngsters navigating the canal in a skiff.

Those canals! They are everywhere. Virgil knew them. Surely it is local scenery with which the *Third Eclogue* ends:

Shut the sluice, lads: the fields have drunk their fill.[21]

Shall we find these canals at swampy Pietole? And is all the scenery in the *Third Eclogue* local? Certain disturbing elements come to mind — but we have not time to adjust them, for Pietro and Diana are conveying us fast to Cremona.

[19]

III. CREMONA

The entrance to Cremona is not particularly impressive, but the Piazza del Commune with its Renaissance loggia, its Romanesque Duomo and its Torrazzo of the thirteenth century, said to be the

FIGURE 12. MARKET AT CREMONA

loftiest tower in Italy, more than efface our disappointment. Moreover, we find a fruit market. A strange gleam comes into Pietro's eye as he steers towards a certain vender. Watermelons, yes, American watermelons! Not quite American, since they are not oblong, but round as a ball. The taste is identical, and most grateful after the journey of the day. The reader may not make them out in the view of the market here given, but if any doubt their existence, I can obtain a written certificate from Pietro. Watermelon is his favorite fruit. He knows when he wants it, which is always, and when and where he has had it.

As we crunch the cool and crimson liquidity, a sudden revelation occurs to me. Pietro's joy is not exceeded by my own. For I can correct all the commentators in the interpretation of a line of Virgil. In the preface to his description of that marvellous garden kept by an old man of Corycia on the banks of the Galaesus, the poet speaks of the *cucumis* that

Winding through the grass
Grows to a belly — [22]

the comfortable τέλος of that vegetable's activity. Following some interpreters, I had always translated *cucumis* by 'cucumber.' Others call it 'gourd.' Much better is Benoist, who declares, "Ce mot désigne ici toutes plantes du même genre, de melon aussi bien que la courge." But this definition is too inclusive. Who will deny that the word means specifically 'watermelon'? [23] The truth came to me when Pietro gave us the Italian for 'watermelon,' namely *cocomero.* 'Cucumber' in Italian is *cetriolo*, quite a different affair. The watermelon is a native of Africa.[24] The learned Naudin remarks that the culture of the melon in Asia is probably as ancient as that of all other alimentary vegetables and that the Greeks and the Romans were doubtless familiar with it, though some forms may have been described as cucumbers.[25] Rather, let us say, *cucumis* in ancient as in modern Italy has never meant anything but watermelon, while in the Dark and Middle Ages, when the luscious fruit, like so many Pagan luxuries, probably disappeared, the barbarians of the North ludicrously misapplied the original name to an ignominious vegetable. The modern Italian for 'cucumber' doubtless comes from a

[21]

vulgar Latin word, a degrading diminutive, *citriolum*, to which Classical authors like Cicero and Virgil did not condescend. The truth has been hidden all these years because no Northern editor of Virgil has ever visited the land of the poet's birth in the month when watermelons are ripe. But now a great light shines on an obscurity, a pleasant line of Virgil has acquired the dignity of epic, and American small boys, particularly those of African origin, like the watermelon itself, can now read the *Georgics* with some sympathy, knowing that their author, when very young, may well have put arms about the best of fruits, abstracted from his father's, or a neighbor's, garden, and have retired for a luscious revel under the shelter of a spreading beech. All this I endeavored to make clear to Pietro, now at work on his third slice, and was gratified to hear him mumble, "Si, Signore, senza dubbio."

Hotel Roma harbored us for the night. Before we went down to dinner, I aimed the camera from our window at a palazzo across the street (Figure 13). It is a not too ancient structure, and yet, in conformity to Italian architectural habits as I have described them above, it is not unworthy of the Renaissance.

We had a good repast in a dining-room truly Roman. It is open to the sky, and with potted plants and statues about the walls suggests an ancient *triclinium*. An awning protects it from sun and showers. My picture (Figure 14) was taken the next morning, when only one waiter was in sight. But if you take notice of one person in Italy — and the kindly Italians like to receive courtesies and to repay them — a little crowd of interested friends soon forms. While I was winding my camera after the view just shown, I had a chance to take another.

[22]

Figure 14. Dining-room of the
Hotel Roma, Cremona

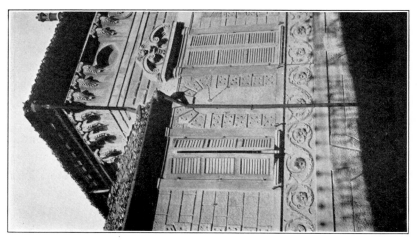

Figure 13. Modern Palazzo
in Cremona

FIGURE 15. THE CULINARY STAFF OF HOTEL ROMA

My helpmate plans a toothsome wayside lunch, which we accumulate from various shops. We literally have to push our way through an enormous crowd. The uninitiated might suspect that a revolution or at least a general strike was in progress, but it is only the big market-day; men have assembled from all the surrounding towns to buy and sell, bargain and discuss, and just stand round. Italians love people, singly and collectively. A treacherous ray of light has nearly spoiled the monumental view that follows of the *Salumeria* of Uberto Grandi, dealer in gastronomic specialties. At least the length of the giraffe-like bottles may be made out, and the dignity of their supporters. The bottles, I must add, were not those that accompanied us on the trip. Pietro knew that better, if smaller, bottles were to be had in country taverns.

[24]

FIGURE 16. *SALUMERIA* AT CREMONA

Among many other things, our proprietor sold a fly-paper called Muiento — a gastronomic specialty of an insidious sort for its devourers. A placard advertised its merits in a fashion hard to beat, or to steal for another language —

NAPOLEONE NON PRESE MOSCA
MUIENTO LE PRENDE TUTTE.

[25]

IV. CREMONA TO MANTUA

We are on the road again. Pietro, anxious to instruct us in all points, stops at a field where rubbish is dumped. It is not dumped and left there. Broken glass is collected and used for making glass again; stones are collected and used for repairing roads; garbage is collected and used for manuring the fields. The magnificent American habit of throwing things away would not be appreciated in Italy. For our part, we might not be so scornful of the profitable pains with which dark-eyed urchins and their mothers poke into the miscellanies of our ash-barrels.

The road is alive this morning. Large white oxen drawing a pear-shaped load of hay look up as we pass. A boy is taking a calf to market in a cart; both of them are protected by a picturesque roof of boughs. Here is a load of corn-leaves; in another cart, a wire basket for eggs, clever contrivance, is suspended from the arched covering and carries its load home safely. Horses in the field wear sheltering caps of white *sole sub ardenti*; in the distance, they look like mediaeval steeds caparisoned for a tourney. Gardens abound, with pole-beans, zucchi and zucchetti, other squashes, the exotic tomato, and the rediscovered *cucumis* or watermelon. Heaps of the latter are often stored in the leaf-shelters. Pietro pulls up at one of them, pointing out that it would make a picturesque photograph (Figure 17).

It does, but his ulterior hopes shall not be gratified. Watermelons should be ice-cold, and there is no ice here. There are heaps of them in the corners of the shelter, where all but one of the numerous family have been discreetly posed in darkness by the photographer. Pietro comes away so sadly that we finally purchase a

FIGURE 17. ROAD-SIDE SHELTER

melon (for fifteen cents); it accompanies us to the city of Virgil's birth, is put on ice and brightens our meal and Pietro's.

Canals line the road as ever. One of them has been lately re-enforced with concrete lining, though it still has its border of small

FIGURE 18. CONCRETE CANAL AND LOCK

plane-trees, whitewashed for further protection. The lock is also of concrete and skilfully made.

Our first objective is the winding River Mella of which Virgil sings in the *Georgics*. By its banks shepherds gather the flower *amellus*, not so much for its beauty — though a thing of beauty it is — as for its medical value when sheep are ailing.[26] We pass Gabbioneta on the way to the River Oglio and Ostiano and note a number of graffiti on a wall. The familiar W IL DUCE (*Viva il Duce*) or W IL FASCIO or W MUSSOLINI, often accompanied by a stencilled image of the great leader's face, have appeared before. Here Mussolini's former secretary, Farinacci receives his applause, and election-appeals are inscribed, like those in ancient Pompeii, as

VOTATE
BERTESI.

A prophet of communism, with the terrifying name of Bombacci, is not treated with the same respect.

ME NE FREGO DI BOMBACCI
E DEL SOL DEL AVEN(IR)

"A fig for Bombacci and his Golden Age to come" — to which a rude figure of the glittering sun is added. Alas, poor Bombacci, he had not learned from the *Fourth Eclogue* that the Age of the Golden Sun was long ago —

tuus iam regnavit Apollo.

We cross the Oglio, not very majestic at that point, and reach Ostiano, meaning to get to the Mella by a short road to the left. But that is in repair, as we learn from a fine-looking old man; his explanations take time, and before he has fairly begun them, we are surrounded by a crowd of inquisitive faces. Our road must lie northward to Pralboino. As the old man utters the word, all fingers point to the way and all voices cry "Pralboino!" "Prabolino," repeats Pietro, wrongly but majestically, and on we go. We pass many vineyards — fields of them. Some of the canals are dry, not that they are exhausted canals but that their water has been temporarily diverted to flood a field. At Pralboino we stop at a trattoria to get that postponed bottle of wine. Pietro conducts the negotiations, addressing us in the formal English tongue, as befits the occasion. A crowd gathers about the car as quickly as the flies swarm into it. Pietro returns with a glass of red and a glass of white for us to try. We make the momentous decision and the purchase is achieved. By this

FIGURE 19. TAVERN BY THE RIVER MELLA AT PRALBOINO

time youths have descended from bicycles and men have halted their carts to witness the ceremony. We wave the throng a good-bye and press on to the River Mella.

Our detour was a happy error; looking for a place for our picnic, we discover the comfortable little inn "Al Ponte," which advertises its attractions in no uncertain terms. We do not enter, but occupy a stone table by the banks of the stream. The hostess brings plates — a luxury that we had not expected. Pietro has his own little table, and votes it an excellent meal.

After the lunch, I clambered down to the level of the stream, hoping to bring back a bunch of *amellus*. I could find nothing to fit what seems the poet's descriptions of it, but caught a view of the river from under the bridge (Figure 21), and later looked down

FIGURE 20. LUNCH BY THE MELLA

from the bridge on the stream, where several row-boats were lazily plying (Figure 22).

We said good-bye to our kindly hosts. The padrone happened to tell us that the people of Pralboino got their wine from Cremona but their bread from Brescia. "It is in the *provincia* of Brescia," he added. "What about Calvisano and Carpenedolo?" I asked. "In what *provincia* are they?" "Likewise in Brescia," he replied. That is interesting news! "Our next town is Asola," I said. "And where is that?" "In the *provincia* of Mantova," was the answer. Here is

FIGURE 22. THE RIVER MELLA FROM
THE BRIDGE

FIGURE 21. THE RIVER MELLA FROM UNDER
THE BRIDGE

food for thought! What are these *provincie*, and what relation do they bear to the ancient townships?

Before reaching Asola we cross the Chiese, a river that must have been dear to Virgil's heart if it is true that his father's estate reached

FIGURE 23. THE RIVER CHIESE NEAR ASOLA

from Carpenedolo down to its banks. Why did he not mention it in his poems? At the time of our visit only a slip of its stream was running, the rest being drained off into the fields.

On coming into Asola we are confronted with the sign PROVINCIA MANTOVANA. The town lies not far from the boundary-line. Thus far our journey has pursued an even tenor. We came on a gentle slope from Milan to Cremona and this slope has continued since then, but thus far has only slightly dropped; Cremona is 47 metres above sea level and Asola 42. We are aiming now at the heart of our quest, at Mantua, but we will approach it from above, to see the Mincio at Goito. We rise a bit to Casaloldo, where we are

FIGURE 24. CHURCH AT CASALOLDO

astonished with a view of the mountains at the north. Mountains may be seen, then, from within the *provincia Mantovana*, and from nearer to the mother-town than Calvisano and Carpenedolo are. I also photograph the church at Casaloldo (Figure 24), hoping that a study of its features might help me to understand Professor Conway's arguments on the architectural similarity of the bell-tower of Calvisano and that of S. Andrea at Mantua.[27] Alas! the pertinence of that argument still remains obscure. On we go, through essentially the same scenery that we traversed the day before. Canals accompany the road as ever, though here and there they are dry, not because the day is hotter — it is, with a clear, dry heat — and because the blazing sun has parched their thirsty throats, but because the waters have been diverted by the hand of man for irrigation. We pass vineyards and fields of mulberry-trees and leafy shelter-huts by the road. There are thick hedges—along one canal a path is lined on both sides with plane-trees. Boys saunter along, with burlap bags over their heads to mitigate the sun — on a wet day those bags will serve as rain-coats. Reeds, suggesting bamboo (and so called the other day by Pietro), grow along the canals and are useful for building shelter-huts and for uniting vine-supports to their trees. Piubega comes and Gazzoldo. At the corner of a field is a shrine with AVE MARIA under the little statue of the Virgin. She stands there blessing the fields as Bacchus did of yore, his images hanging from pine-branches, swaying in the breeze, and fructifying hollow valleys, deep glades,

And whereso'er he turns his honest face.[28]

We are on good Roman territory now, the ancient Via Postumia, and it is taking us to Goito. Vines and vines — more than on the way from Milan to Cremona. Flourishing crops as before. The tower of a church at Goito looms up in the straight road when we are about two miles away — so the shepherds in the *Ninth Eclogue* described the

FIGURE 25. THE RIVER MINCIO AT GOITO

FIGURE 25A. THE RIVER MINCIO AT GOITO

tomb of Bianor, founder of Mantua, when they had made half of their journey to town.

The immediate charm of Goito for us was Virgil's most beloved stream, the River Mincio. Perhaps for this association it appealed to us more than those that we had seen earlier in the day. Figures 25 and 25A, joined, give a complete view looking up stream. The growth at the right is reeds, suggesting bamboo and serving its purpose. They can be even better seen in the next picture. Again the

FIGURE 26. REEDS IN THE MINCIO AT GOITO

Third Eclogue comes to mind. Two shepherds, met for a contest in song, are exchanging ribald banter, and the one says derisively of the other, "And you hid behind the reeds!" This is the retort ridiculous. The reeds would grow in swampy land or by a riverbank. The rustic, who had filched a goat, was hard pressed to take refuge in such a desperate spot. Reeds have become more abundant as we have advanced — I wonder if they will be thick at Calvisano.

Right by our stopping-place is a worthy monument to the Bersaglieri who stemmed the tide of the Austrian advance in 1848. The

FIGURE 27. VILLA GIRAFFA AT GOITO

monument, erected in 1926, bears the following inscriptions, below a spirited figure of a Bersagliere with his waving cock-plume.

QVI
COI BERSAGLIERI DI LA MARMORA
LA VITTORIA ITALIANA
METTEVA LE PENNE

LE "FIAMME ROSSE" DI MANTOVA
COMPIVTA LA GESTA DEI PADRI
ERESSERO IL MONVMENTO

VIII APRILE MDCCCXLVIII
XX SETTEMBRE MCMXXVI

IN QUEST OF VIRGIL'S BIRTHPLACE

We were lucky for still another reason in our stopping-place, for we were at the gates of the Villa Giraffa (Fig. 27). At first we thought it a hotel, but a courteous servant of the place enlightened us. He pointed to a tall pole with a giraffe at its summit, and showed us an inscription on the outer wall.

> HOSPES SALVE
> HOSTIS CAVE
> "Friend, come in!
> Foe, look out!"

On the rear wall shown above is a Renaissance fresco of lords and ladies hunting with the falcon. That, too, has its inscription, which spells out acrostically the name of the villa, designates its owners, the Gozzi Fumagalli, and honors the Mincio that runs by its borders.

> GRATO
> INTVITV
> REFOVET
> ACCOLAS
> FVMAGALLIANOS
> FAVSTVS
> AMNIS

In front of this wall is a delightful court with flowers and a fountain, athwart which can be seen the façade of the outer wing (Figure 28). Our guide also showed us a little chapel, with faded frescoes of the fourteenth century. In the rear is a bit of woods — a *"bosco"* — with little fish-ponds and plentiful vines. A modern attraction is a tennis-court, by the edge of the Mincio — modern, yet the great patron of Virgil and of Horace played the ancient equivalent of our game, from which the poets, for different ailments, were excused.[29]

FIGURE 30. CANAL AT MARMIROLO

FIGURE 28. VILLA GIRAFFA AT GOITO

We have kept Diana waiting long, but at last we are on the road to Mantua. In coming to Goito we have gradually descended to 30 metres, but we are not aware of the fact till we consult the map. We know that in Mantua we shall be as low as 18, and are ready any moment to close eyes, and noses, as we plunge into that

FIGURE 29. FARM AT MARMIROLO

Slough of Despond that Professor Conway's map might lead one to expect.[30] Curiously, as we spin on, the feeling is no different from what it has been at the start — easy travel over a good road at a virtually continuous level; the slope has been sure, but slow. The vegetation is what we have seen all along. Same trees, same vines (only more of them), same vegetables, same fruit including water-melons (*deliciae Petri*), same hedges and the same canals, some with the more elaborate sort of stone sluice. An attractive little farmhouse at Marmirolo, half-way down from Goito, has its own canal, which joins that at the side of the road (Figure 30). Nor is there an absence of canals as we proceed. Some of them are dry. Their water, which now comes from the Mincio, has been diverted into the fields.

Shut the sluice, lads; the fields have drunk their fill.

Yes, we can sing that verse in Mantua — however, Pietole remains to be seen. Thus far, at any rate, our journey is all of a piece.

FIGURE 31. MANTUA FROM THE PONTE DEI MOLINI

We now catch a splendid view of the city across the lagoon; now we rumble across the covered bridge, Ponte dei Molini, with its clattering mill and its little niches occupied by statues of saints; and now we are at last in Virgil's city. It is a cleanly place and we have seen it by a beautiful approach. We drive to the Aquila d'Oro, where we are ready for the evening meal, *cucumis* included.

V. MANTUA

Mantua is a stately city of no little charm. The Mincio, a small-
ish stream before, now broadens into three lagoons, the Lago Superiore, the Lago di Mezzo and the Lago Inferiore. The city pro-
trudes into these lagoons from the south, and is connected with the

FIGURE 32. PIAZZA SORDELLO FROM THE PALAZZO DUCALE

opposite bank by two main bridges, the Ponte dei Molini, over which
we entered, and the Ponte S. Georgio, from which the view of the
city, as we later find, is even more impressive. It is these bridges that
divide the Lago di Mezzo and the Lago Inferiore from each other and
from the Lago Superiore; in other words the division of one large
lagoon into three parts is artificial. (See Map 3.)

[43]

IN QUEST OF VIRGIL'S BIRTHPLACE

For lovers of good art, particularly that of Mantegna, and of fine old buildings, Mantua abounds in delights. A visit to the Palazzo Ducale in the Piazza Sordello transports one to the chivalrous, and bloodthirsty, days of the Gonzaga and the Bonacolsi in the fourteenth century, while the Palazzo Cadenazzi with its Torre della Gabbia, crowned by an iron cage in which condemned prisoners were once exposed, has a greater antiquity still. In the Piazza Erbe nearby is a graceful house of the fourteenth century, once the palace of the merchant Boniforte (Figure 33).

These and other attractions compensate for the natural disadvantages of the site. Mantua is flat. Mantua is hot. Mantua is hospitable to mosquitoes. The bed in our chamber was provided with a stately white canopy of mosquito-netting enclosing it completely. It was a neat mosquito trap, keeping fifty out and three within, the three that a training in nimbleness and wariness had best fitted to survive. One of the minor poems attributed by some to Virgil sings of the heroism of a mosquito. Visitors to Mantua have reason to believe this poem genuine. By day the city sleeps. Men and women are at work behind curtains of burnt umber. By night it wakes. The cafés opposite our hotel are thronged; tables and chairs are thrust out into the narrow street. We stroll over to this Mantuan night club, order coffee and start a game of cards. The waiter courteously informs us that to continue it we must take a table within. Games of cards lead to discussion and discussion to infractions of the peace — better to break the peace indoors than without. We decide not to break it at all; indeed we have enough to do in watching the human comedy about us.

Mantua is flat, but Mantua has views. In a painting by Domenico Morone in the Palazzo Ducale representing a conflict of the

FIGURE 33. PALAZZO DEL MERCANTE BONIFORTE
IN THE PIAZZA ERBE

Gonzaga and the Bonacolsi, mountains appear in the background. "What are those?" we ask. "Why those are the mountains back of

[45]

Verona." "But why put them in this Mantuan scene?" "Because they can be seen from Mantua on a clear day." Here is news! Young Virgil, if he had the spirit of adventure — and his creative imagination was adventurous if anybody's ever was — might have followed this glimpse of distant peaks till he saw what mountains were. I am supposing, for the moment, that he was born at Pietole and knew the city Mantua.

VI. PIETOLE

We needed a full morning for the Palazzo Ducale — and we needed more. The noon-time was broiling, but those in search of Virgil's birthplace mind no heat. We started soon after lunch for Pietole. The southward road, lined with tall poplars, is like many that we have traversed thus far. There is nothing particularly marshy that we can see. We pass a girl on a bicycle and a boy on a donkey. No canals yet — oh, here they are! We breathe a sigh of relief. They are necessary even in the "swamp." The roadside growth is heavy at times. In Virgil's day there may well have been woods in many of the districts through which we have passed. Fruit-trees are noticeable, though here as elsewhere they have made a losing fight against the profitable mulberry and Gran Turco. Pines and cypresses may be seen in the garden of a villa. We find no beech-trees, nor have we seen any on the previous days. Pietro, we remember, knows them, farther to the north. They might have figured conspicuously in the woodland about Mantua in Virgil's day. They are not the sort fittest to survive in a region gradually given over to the cultivation of useful crops.

[46]

FIGURE 35. STATUE OF VIRGIL AT PIETOLE

FIGURE 34. STATUE OF VIRGIL AT PIETOLE

So this is Pietole! It is a tiny village, conspicuous chiefly for the Osteria Virgilio and the little park that holds his monument. I had made a pilgrimage to this place in 1913. I could not then or on the present visit obtain a good photograph of the statue, which fascinated me much. The reader will find at least a suggestion in the views that are given here (Figures 34 and 35) and below (Figure 126).

Opposite the park is the Osteria, whose title on the façade almost vanished in the blazing sun. Views of the interior were attempted, with little success. This was a pity, for the proprietor and his wife and numerous friends had posed in characteristic attitudes — but they could not retain their attitudes long enough for a time-exposure. The proprietress I was determined to take, so I stationed her by a table in the garden, with a long line of her relatives and friends looking contentedly at the camera outside the focus. My object was scientific. It was to show, for the benefit of those that accept as Virgil's the minor poems that have come down under his name, that the theme of *Copa*, the Barmaid, is not without analogies near Mantua today.

On the map here shown, it will be seen that various names suggest the memory of Virgil. There are *la Virgiliana* and *Pietole vecchia* besides the modern hamlet. One might pick up legends about the poet by inquiring discreetly at any of these places. Conway shows a view of a certain *fondo Virgilio* which challenges attention.[31] Attracted by the title *Pietole vecchia*, I urged Pietro to find it. On the way we passed a little brick oven outside a farm. The baking oven is within the house; this one without is used for heating water for washing clothes, which are rinsed in the canal nearby (Figure 38).

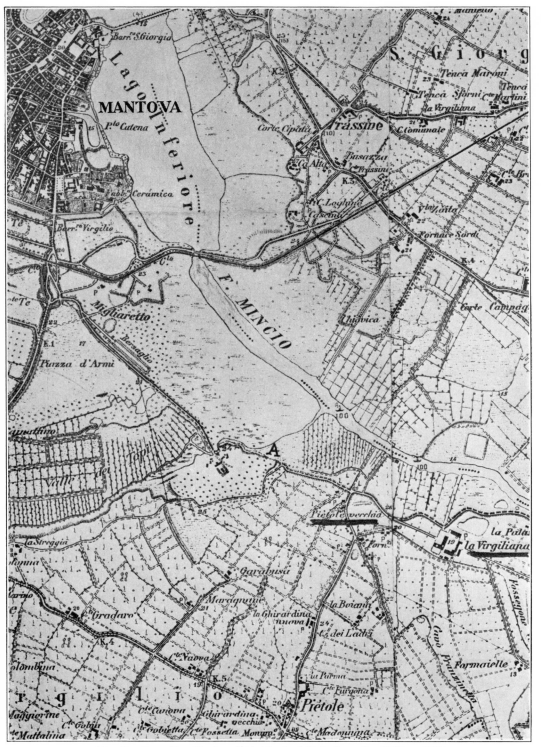

MAP 2. *From Map No. 2, published by the Istituto Geografico Militare, 1885.*

FIGURE 37. *COPA MANTOVANA*

FIGURE 36. VIRGIL'S *POPINA* AT PIETOLE

FIGURE 38. OVEN NEAR PIETOLE

FIGURE 39. AN INDUSTRIOUS FAMILY NEAR PIETOLE

Other canals are dry; their water is in use at the moment. Here is a field well dotted with fine black heaps of manure, all ready to be worked into the ground. Further on a weaver at her task consents to

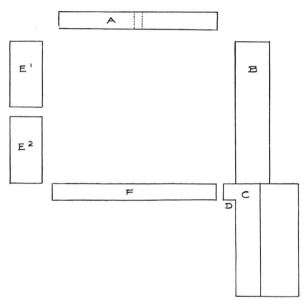

FIGURE 40. *LA VIRGILIANA*

interrupt it while the camera is at work — the other inmates of the house are partly set forth here (Figure 39).

Pietole vecchia is hard to find. It is the real Pietole, but was destroyed in the early part of the nineteenth century, and today is a name on the map — *stat parvi nominis umbra* — representing a tradition rather than a centre discoverable today. But *La Virgiliana*

[51]

FIGURE 41. *IL COLUMBARIO* AT *LA VIRGILIANA*

FIGURE 42. *IL CORTILE* AT *LA VIRGILIANA*

exists, a bit of which Conway apparently caught in his picture called *fondo Virgilio.* It is an interesting establishment, the proprietor of

FIGURE 43. WITHIN *IL CORTILE*

which was glad to exhibit it. Once it was a noble estate, belonging to the Gonzaga; one of the buildings contains a wall as old as the fourteenth century. I append a rude plan (Figure 40). We must think out of the way the modern house (F), which covers the site of the ancient entrance. We may reconstruct in imagination an avenue lined with cypresses such as is pictured later (Figure 90), leading up to the main dwelling (A), now called *Il Columbario* (Figure 41).

FIGURE 44. HAY-BARN AND END OF *IL CORTILE* AT *LA VIRGILIANA*

The road goes on under the tower and continues to the Mincio. In the foreground one may discern an industrious woman well laden with the results of her washing. On the right of this building, as we face it, is that called the Cortile (B), with crenellated roofs at the ends (Figure 42). Today it harbors many oxen and cows and many pigs, whose restless nature somewhat spoiled a time-exposure (Figure 43). The outer part of the building beyond (C) is well stacked with hay; this is a bountiful farm (Figure 44).

FIGURE 46. RACKS FOR MULBERRY LEAVES
AND SILKWORMS AT *LA VIRGILIANA*

FIGURE 45. AN ANCIENT CORNER AT
LA VIRGILIANA

The other side of this building is the most obviously ancient part, retaining stone-work of the fourteenth century (Figure 45). In a room within there are remains of stucco work, including a portrait. It had other uses in the days of the Gonzaga; today it contains racks

FIGURE 47. ANCIENT MONASTERY AT *LA VIRGILIANA*

spread with mulberry leaves, and silkworms feeding on them. Time-exposures, once more, are difficult in Italy (Figure 46).

On the other side of the main court, the buildings E¹ and E² once formed part of a monastery; now, like all the original structures of the estate, they are put to menial uses (Figure 47). As we came away, we saw outside the Cortile (B) a pair of stately oxen harnessed to a wine cart, worthy a place among the white herds of which Virgil sang.[32] Their keepers are by them; the proprietor was too modest to join the group (Figure 48).

The Gonzaga family, if they chose the name *La Virgiliana*, evidently accepted the traditions that Virgil was born somewhere nearby. Could they possibly have chosen the very site to which tradition had also assigned the villa of Virgil's family? And might it

FIGURE 48. OXEN AT *LA VIRGILIANA*

not have been really there, rebuilt from time to time with increasing magnificence, even as Horace's Sabine villa was enlarged by later owners? I will leave these questions without answers, since Pietro and Diana decide that it is time to make our way back to town.[33]

On the return, we were especially impressed with the luxuriant vines. Their supports as ever are mulberry trees, instead of the ancient elm or poplar. The tree is generally low. Young Americans reading Latin poetry may imagine that the elm to which the vine was wedded attained the height of a New England elm, in the crest of which the vine and its products would be lost to view. Horace may be partly responsible for the error with his verses on the happy farmer who wedded the thrifty vine-shoots to tall poplar-trees.[34] Perhaps he is speaking of relative heights in stock terms, for the vine, as

FIGURE 49. VINES NEAR PIETOLE

such, is lowly and the poplar, as such, is tall. Sometimes, moreover, we note a tree of considerable height. Beyond the line of trees, poles are set in obliquely and are connected with the trees by withes plucked from the sedges. The vine is thus invited to clamber to the supports and hence to spread its surface (Figure 50).

The pruner of the vine and the tiller of the field are refreshed with a drink of water now and then, and though in pastorals they seek a cool spring bubbling forth in a sheltered glen, I imagine that even in

Virgil's day they may have been served in the practical, though by no means prosaic, fashion prevalent today (Figure 51).

Possibly some of the views here shown will suggest to the reader that the country about Pietole is not entirely a marsh. It differs in

FIGURE 50. VINES AND THEIR SUPPORTS, NEAR PIETOLE

no essential aspect from what we have noted on the road from Milan to Mantua. We see the marsh as we proceed; it does not extend any great distance from the river-banks. At the time of my visit in May, 1913, I was much more impressed with the swampy character of the surroundings of the city. Possibly there was some overflow of the river at that earlier season of the year. But possibly my eye may have been attracted by some field flooded artificially from a canal, like those that we saw at several points on our journey. At Pietole

FIGURE 51. VINES, DONKEY AND WATER-CART NEAR PIETOLE

itself I cannot imagine that conditions are essentially different in any part of the year from what we saw in August.

We are pursuing the small road leading from *La Virgiliana* to the town, and have arrived somewhere near the point marked A on

Map 2 (p. 48). It is the half-way point of our journey back. All at once the dome of the cathedral and other prominent edifices in the city are conspicuous over the marshes, even as they are in the view of the lagoon shown above in Figure 31. Was this the path taken by the shepherds of the *Ninth Eclogue* when they descried the tomb of Bianor at the half-way point? The incident in the eclogue, of course, harks back to Theocritus's *Seventh Idyll*, in which the shepherds, strolling along to the harvest festival, pass the tomb of Brasilas at the half-way point.[35] That is no proof that the tomb of Bianor is a fiction of our poet. Bianor was the founder of Mantua and is mentioned by Virgil elsewhere.[36] That a tomb had been erected to his memory is most natural to suppose. That it stood just without the city in the place regularly taken for the cemetery in ancient times — witness the Dipylon Gate at Athens and the Appian Way in Rome — is likewise something probable. Wherever the ancient road ran from Pietole it might well have afforded a view of the sepulchre two miles or so away — either Pietole or *La Virgiliana* is something over three miles away. Surely Mantua was the town for which Virgil's shepherds were aiming, and just as surely they could not have descried the tomb of Bianor fifteen miles off, the half-way point to Calvisano.[37]

Shortly after passing Point A, we lose the view of Mantua across the lagoon.[38] We come to a fort called San Virgilio. Could it be San Vigilio? I asked Pietro several times and each time he sounded the *r* with greater distinctness. Canonization at last! What else can you expect of people who think that our poet was born at Pietole? The fort is an ancient edifice.[39] It played its part in the war with the Austrians, but in the Great War served merely as a store-house for ammunition. It has still sufficient military importance to prohibit the taking of photographs. Pietro, as an old soldier, warned me against that. Nor was it for me to disobey such warning, especially when I saw a sentry, pacing the wall, look carefully over in our direction.

We have come to the marshes. They are not always dismal and not always soaked. They bear a goodly crop, perhaps several crops,

FIGURE 52. HAYING ON THE MANTUAN MARSHES

of hay. A load was coming in as we drove by. The sight of the meadow and its yield suggested opulence, not desolation. The very reeds of the marsh are profitable, not only in the construction of leaf-shelters and vine supports, but for making seats of chairs. There also grows with them an herb called *treghole* — if I got the name right — the fruit of which is good to eat, with a taste like that of chestnuts. This information was given to Pietro by a man on the road who

FIGURE 53. THE NEW STATUE OF VIRGIL
IN THE *PIAZZA VIRGILIANA*

scrambled down to the brink to find a specimen. He was gone so
long that we did not await his return. Mine the lack of patience —
we had had a strenuous jaunt on a hot day. We come to the part of

[63]

the swamp that is covered with water. Two machines are coursing it, cleaning out the slimy growth. If our American method of sprinkling Paris green over marshes from an aeroplane were adopted, Mantua could be cleared of its mosquitoes. The marsh now yields to the lagoon — and that too is profitable, as the presence of several fishers attests. Washerwomen are plying their task; the finished product is drying in the sun. We cross by the Ponte San Giorgio — an even more impressive approach than that by which we came in yesterday.

The day cannot close without a visit to the new statue of Virgil in his own *Piazza Virgiliana* (Figure 53). The monument replaces that destroyed by Carlo Malatesta in the fourteenth century. The statue is of bronze set on a high marble pedestal. It is the last work of the sculptor Quadrelli, who died before the final casting was done. On either side of the wide platform are allegorical groups representing epic and pastoral poetry; a young sculptor of Mantua, Menozzi, is their creator. On the front of the monument one reads

A VIRGILIO
LA PATRIA

and around the base are placed Dante's lines

TV SE' COLVI DA CVI IO TOLSI
LO BELLO STILE CHE M'HA FATTO ONORE.

The better of the two allegorical figures is that representing pastoral poetry. Even so, it is something of a medley. As a whole, the monument lacks the simple beauty of that at Pietole. However, it is not without dignity, and the Piazza itself, when the landscape-gardening now in progress has been completed, will make a worthy tribute of the city to its poet. The view here given of the rear of the park was taken about a third of the way down from the statue.

In any case, it is gratifying to feel that age after age pays its homage to the poet in Mantua. The tribute made in the fourteenth cen-

FIGURE 54. *PIAZZA VIRGILIANA*

tury takes a different form from what it does today. What pleases one epoch may seem absurd to the next. Just this human shame of the ridiculous will presumably keep the poet's fame perennial in stone.

This has been a memorable day. We return with the conviction that something still may be said for little Pietole as the spot where our poet was born.

[65]

VII. MANTUA TO BRESCIA

Early next morning we are ready for the most exciting experience of all — for we are to look upon scenery appropriate for the author of the *Eclogues*. We lay in supplies for our lunch at the market in the Piazza Erbe, visiting a *salumeria* for a paté and a *drogheria* for alcohol for our little heater — indispensable companion of a well-regulated journey. Pietro defines nicely the difference between *salumeria* and *drogheria* — to one familiar with an American grocery, the distinction sounds a bit scholastic. What odds if you get what you want? And why pother about words when a handsome lad from the *drogheria* after conducting us to a pastry-shop and back, blushingly refuses a tip? I have had this experience once before in Europe, and again it was in Italy, at the library in Verona, when a boy commissioned by the genial (and comfort-loving) librarian to escort me to the closed library and wait over hours till I finished my work, drew back with feelings somewhat hurt from the two lire — about a half-dollar then — in my outstretched hand.

So good-bye to Mantua! We skirt the southern edge of the Lago Superiore. A canal by the road is dry. The fields are rich in tilth and vines. There is the great swamp, but it is a thing apart from the fields. The road is being repaired in American fashion with a crashing juggernaut and streams of tar. We stop to see the Romanesque church at Le Grazie at the end of the lagoon. I *must* photograph a splendid type of Mother Italy, matron worthy of the days of Caesar and Augustus, fit parent of the conquerors of the world —

Romanos rerum dominos gentemque togatam.

Not all of her gets into the photograph, but the loss is more than compensated by the autochthonous group that forms while the camera is adjusted. I have taken all Rome as well as its symbol. Oh frieze on the *Ara Pacis*, look to your laurels!

All aboard! We leave the marsh and are bound for the heights. The ground rises perceptibly, but only perceptibly (*sensim*) as we

FIGURE 55. OUTSIDE THE CHURCH AT LE GRAZIE

proceed. On a gentle slope of this kind, it is easier to tell when you are mounting than when you descend. We have reached 28 metres at Le Grazie, 30 at Rivalta, 31 at Rodigo, but on the whole the effect of the ride is as before — travel at an even tenor on a good and level road. Fertile fields as ever; in one of them, motor-ploughs are stirring the soil. Virgil would have put them into a poem. He was no sentimentalist when it came to science and machinery — he turned into epic the great engineering feat of his day, the union of the two lakes at Baiae into a land-locked harbor, even though one of them bordered on the dreadful descent to Avernus.

On the outskirts of Rodigo there are thick clumps of trees — well might there have been stretches of woodland in Virgil's time. We

FIGURE 56. CASTEL GOFFREDO

pass a handsome *scuola communale*, a modern building in the ancient style. I am reminded that in Mantua I noted a *Scuola elementare Virgiliana*. Villa Cappella and San Lazzaro slip by and Ceresara with a fine old gate. It is a wonderfully cool day — it can be cool even in Mantua — with some prospect of rain. Full canals, rows of plane-trees, leafy shelters — everything as before. A gentle shower falls, but Diana shakes it from her speeding shoulders and out comes the sun. Castel Goffredo, at an elevation of 56 metres, is a clean little town. I pause to take a picture of the campanile — for what architectural evidence it may contain — and of a crenellated tower.

The street now runs between tall plane-trees. The road is as good as ever, and is, as ever, accompanied by canals. We enter Casalpoglio with a thrill, for from here came one of the two inscriptions im-

FIGURE 57. OXEN AT ACQUAFREDDA

portant for the identification of Virgil's birth-place.[40] The campanile attracts us, but nothing else is worthy of note. On beyond, the fields luxuriate in tobacco — not a Virgilian, and not an Horatian, crop. Curious freak of history, for Horace was born for a smoke. However did he get on without one? Casalpoglio is our last town within the *provincia* of Mantua. We cross the border into that of Brescia and at Acquafredda pass a group of oxen by the canal. They apparently have just found out that the place is well named.

As we near Carpenedolo, shooting up to the north, we come in sight of the famous ridge. Professor Conway is right. It is the first elevation of the kind that one meets on the way from Mantua to Brescia. I should have aimed my camera at it from the point where we saw it first, but I wait for a better view, and with the ill luck that

FIGURE 58. THE RIDGE AT CARPENEDOLO

often befalls the amateur photographer, wait too long. By mounting a wall I at least can catch the tip of the crest, but in August the way-side growth hides what is between. The reader will get a better idea of the ridge from Conway's illustration.[41] Looking at the canal as we pass along, we note the spot well selected by Conway for his picture.[42] The stream is not so broad nearer the town; here it is at a picturesque point (Figure 59). We approach the entrance to the town and pass through the gate (Figure 62).

[70]

FIGURE 59. CANAL AT CARPENEDOLO

FIGURE 60. APPROACH TO CARPENEDOLO

The cravings of the inner man suggest that the hour for luncheon has come. Pietro intimates as much. But first we must explore the ridge a bit, and, if we can, find Virgil's pastoral scenery there. We ascend as far as Diana thinks it best to fly, and after a talk with some kindly peasants, we impress into our service a diminutive guide,

FIGURE 61. *GUIDO IL GUIDA*

named Guido. *Guido il guida! Nomen et omen.* He will show us the way. We mount by a path and steps of stone to the terrace of the little church of Santa Maria. Half-way up we look through the gate to the houses below and the distant plain (Figure 63). Attaining the terrace, we have the church of San Giovanni and its cypresses in the foreground and a wide view of the houses in the plain and the ridge on beyond (Figure 64). Back of us is a ruined tower, which played its part in the old conflict with the Austrians. Surely there is

FIGURE 63. TERRACE OF SANTA MARIA
AT CARPENEDOLO

FIGURE 62. TOWER-GATE AT
CARPENEDOLO

height enough here to enable a shepherd in the valley to see his goats hanging on a cliff and to note the shadows of evening lengthen from the high hills. And grottoes? Virgil's rustics as well as those of Theocritus know them, and both Mr. Conway and his friend Mr. Hallam, happy proprietor of what may have been Horace's villa at Tivoli,[43] have found "grottoes of sorts" at several points on the

FIGURE 64. SAN GIOVANNI, CARPENEDOLO

ridge.[44] Our time did not permit an extensive ramble, but here, for instance (Figure 65), is a depression amid a sheltering clump of trees that in a happier age of gold might, with a little refashioning, have invited the shepherd when the sun blazed at noon-time. Then, there was a spring of cold water bubbling from the rocks. Now, its flow is caught in a modern pipe with a faucet, embedded in an artificial wall. Just after the picture was taken, a peasant filled his bucket there. Beeches? We find none. Nor elms. But both might have been there in Virgil's day. Cypresses and pines we have discovered. They seem, as at Pietole, the result of special cultivation, but they may well have been more abundant long ago.

Pietro is displaying an heroic restraint, and we must exercise it a bit longer till we see the Chiese. Virgil's farm, according to Professor

FIGURE 65. "GROTTO" AT CARPENEDOLO

Conway, extended from some point on the ridge — for it is precisely here that, as the shepherd in the *Ninth Eclogue* says, "the hills melt into the plain" — and this sloped gently to the aged beeches and the water.[45] So we make for the Chiese, since it cannot be far off. It proves farther than we expected — a good two kilometres away![46] Most of its ample current had been drained off for the fields. The view up the stream and the view down show ribbons of water slipping through a gravelly field, the natural bed of the stream, while from the bridge beyond almost nothing is seen but an expanse of stones.

Really, it *is* time for luncheon, which we take under the trees by a road-side canal. I prove a sullen table-companion, for my thoughts are busy with doubtings. A farm extending a mile and a quarter!

FIGURE 66. THE RIVER CHIESE NEAR CARPENEDOLO

Not impossible dimensions for an estate, either then or now. But is that what Tityrus in the *First Eclogue* possessed? Rather we see there a place of modest dimensions — *modus agri, non ita magnus.*[47] Part of its soil is rocky and part infested with the marsh. But its very poverty wards off too many neighbors; its sheep do not catch contagion from an adjoining flock.[48] At least there is pleasant slumber prompted by the buzzing bees in the hedge-row and by "the moan of doves in immemorial elms." And above all, it is the shepherd's own.

FIGURE 67. THE RIVER CHIESE NEAR CARPENEDOLO

FIGURE 68. THE RIVER CHIESE NEAR CARPENEDOLO

He has gone all the way from Mantua [49] to Rome, and the youthful deity to whom he appealed there has vouchsafed him the sure possession of his little farm. But where was it? Rocky fields might do for Calvisano, but what of the marsh-land? Does not the mention of marshes transport us to Pietole? And what about the familiar streams on the banks of which Tityrus loved to be? According to Professor Conway they were either the Chiese and the Mella or the Chiese and the Mincio. The shortest straight line from Carpenedolo to the Mella measures over $23\frac{1}{2}$ kilometres, or $14\frac{1}{2}$ miles [50] and the distance to the Mincio is not less. No tired shepherd, wishing to lie down *inter nota flumina*, walks fourteen miles for the purpose. Virgil's streams are on, or by, Tityrus's little farm.[51] Possibly we need not think of the mightier rivers; picturesque little canals would serve the purpose, nor would the poet's plural *flumina* require more than one of them. If we must be definite, I cannot believe that Tityrus's stream is, or his streams are, anything else than the Mincio.[52]

And no, we may not be too definite. Definite touches of description there are in Virgil's pastorals, and exquisite bits of realistic detail in the midst of scenery that throughout is essentially ideal. A mind like Virgil's could not work so precisely, so pedantically, as to contrive a local setting, a native setting, for his odd-numbered eclogues and imaginary scenery for those with even numbers. Are all the scenes local in the *Fifth Eclogue*? One may, perhaps, call the Carpenedolo ridge a mountain and find holes in its sides that might serve for grottoes. But is it here that the dead Daphnis, brother-shepherd of the singers, used to roam? Daphnis is mourned by African lions as well as by the mountains and the woods. He yoked Armenian tigers to his chariot and brought on Bacchanalian troupes with vine-encircled wands. Wild doings for little Andes! When Daphnis died, Pales, ay Apollo himself left the fields, — the fields of Calvisano and Carpenedolo? Now that Daphnis is translated to the skies, he sends down, good lover of peace, a bit of the Golden Age; the wolf plots no treachery for the flock and the hunter sets no snare for the deer — just thirty miles northwest of the city of Mantua! No, no! This way madness lies. Shall Julius Caesar be confined to Andes? Rather, we must admit the incongruities in Virgil's pastoral scene, and admit that they are harmonized by his harmonizing imagination. It is the same imagination that plays delicately with pastoral names and contemporary allusions, contriving mazes and culs-de-sac for those who would track out his allegories by rigid paths.[53] Virgil's art is impressionistic and suggestive. It forbids us to look too nicely for this or that person and this or that place. Verily, the entourage of Carpenedolo cannot supply what his fancy saw and his art set forth with a truth independent of topography.

I am aroused from these heresies — has the noon-day devil bewitched me, or the sly influence of Pietolian wine? — by the reminder that we have not yet seen Calvisano. Across the Chiese, the landscape reverts to its usual features. No ridges are here — the country is flat. Prosperous fields, way-side canals, mulberry-trees and all the rest. Not far from the town we come to a church with a cemetery; and here Pietro halts. During the War he had stopped at the house of the cemetery-keeper, which adjoins the church; the place has fond associations for him (Figure 69).

I stationed Pietro and his friend by a well in the little court-yard and present them both here, taking the chance to express our appreciation of our guide's abounding cheerfulness and his helpful information, without which there would be many a gap in the present narrative (Figure 70).

The greeting over, we take to the road again. At several points along the canal, there are concrete reënforcements, locks of the new

FIGURE 69. PIETRO'S QUARTERS NEAR CALVISANO

style, and now and then a little bridge (Figure 71). Just outside Calvisano is a Romanesque church, with the town bell-tower peering over not far away (Figure 72). We draw near to the tower itself, and inasmuch as I have stopped to take a picture of it, we find by the time we reach the gate that we are making a triumphal entry between rows of most of the citizens of Calvisano, at the hour of half-past three (Figure 73). A small boy gets in the way. "Òca, òca!" cries Pietro — and the goose jumps aside in a fright.

Figure 71. CANAL BRIDGE NEAR CALVISANO

Figure 70. PIETRO AND HIS FRIEND

We fall to thinking, again, of the architecture of this tower — a tour d'horloge and part, it would seem, of the ancient wall — in relation to the bell-tower of the church of Sant' Andrea at Mantua. After much thought, we still fail to appreciate the clear traits of a

FIGURE 72. OUTSKIRTS OF CALVISANO

family likeness — traits, that is, not shared by many bell-towers in North Italy. More impressive evidence is suddenly presented by an alluring sign on the wall of a trattoria

AL CANTV́ EL VI LE BV́.

Pietro renders this bit of dialect into court Italian, with the meaning

At Corner Inn
The wine's not thin.

El vi le bú, he explains, is Brescian for *il vino e buono* — a statement later corroborated by an American expert.[54] Brescian, not Mantuan!

FIGURE 73. THE BELL TOWER OF CALVISANO

Dialect is a good test. Furthermore, in the modern apportionment of the *provincie*, both Carpenedolo and Calvisano, as we have learned from our host by the Mella, belong not to Mantua but to Brescia. The maps (1 and 3) will make it plain. Of course we do not know what the ancient limits of the township of Mantua were, and we will not deny that a place might be 30 miles away and yet within a township. But the present boundary, even though this has not been invariable in modern times,[55] and the present dialect should incline one to assign the two villages to the ancient Brescia and not to the ancient Mantua, unless strong proof to the contrary can be adduced. Moreover, if we are reckoning exactly with the exact Probus, it is Calvisano that is exactly 30 Roman miles away [56] and not Carpenedolo, which is not quite 25. And yet it is at Carpenedolo and not at Calvisano that Professor Conway would locate Virgil's farm. For this, considering the scenery, there is reason. The terrain at Calvisano is of course at a higher elevation than that at Pietole (63 metres) but in itself it is just as level. There is no ridge, as at Carpenedolo. To be sure, the Brescian Alps — not particularly picturesque — are visible on the horizon [57] and on especially clear days the snowy peaks beyond them may be descried. But the shadows that fall from the distant Brescian hills cannot be of much account in the twilight of Calvisano, and if a shepherd of the latter place wished to see a goat hanging from the crag, he would have to foot it over ten miles to the north. If we choose Carpenedolo, then, we must admit that Probus was not quite exact. And what becomes of the inscriptions, neither of which was found at Carpenedolo?

Our thoughts become more and more unsettled as we stroll about in Calvisano, a pleasant little place, traversed by those sheltering arcades that delight one in so many Italian towns, lineal descendants of the ancient *porticus* and ancestors of the modern *gallerie*, stretch-

FIGURE 75. VINEYARD NEAR
CASTENEDOLO

FIGURE 74. ROCKY FIELD AND CONCRETE
CANAL NEAR CALVISANO

ing their branches to right and to left, obviating the use of an umbrella and providing centres for shopping, strolling, dining, and wining.

But it is time to complete the journey to Brescia. We mount again and skim the level road. Some of the fields are dry; Gran

FIGURE 76. THE BRESCIAN ALPS FROM CASTENEDOLO

Turco and other crops in them are withered and small. Some fields are rocky and yield nothing. Here is one about three miles from Calvisano (Figure 74).

But look again! Gangs of workmen are clearing the stones away, and beautiful concrete canals are in process of construction. Give the great Ruler time, and irrigation will make this part of Italy as glad with the laughing corn as the other fields by which we have passed. No doubt stony fields could be found in Virgil's day at Carpenedolo

— perhaps even at flat Pietole. The accumulated industry of the ages has cleared the rocks away and is now attending to those that remain.

Only comparatively few fields on the way to Brescia lack irrigation and fertility. There are beautiful vineyards covering the hillsides with rows of pines for borders. Especially fine is one near Castenedolo, about five and a half miles from the city (Figure 75).

And now we have our first impressive view of the foothills of the Alps by Brescia. Here one might think of shadows falling from lofty mountains, though for a view of hanging goats one would need a powerful spy-glass.

We are on the last lap. The women that we pass wear shawls more frequently than in the other towns that we have seen. There is something ancient and Roman in their bearing. I remember years ago at Verona the dignity of the men's cloaks, one end flung over the left shoulder in Roman style; they gave the wearer, as he posed in an arcade, an air of majesty and aloofness. We enter Brescia.

VIII. BRESCIA

Following the impeccable Muirhead, in his English edition of the *Guide Bleu*, we had picked out as our hotel the *Gallo*, starred and "well spoken of." Pietro had his doubts. He recommended the *Igea Terminus*, the most sumptuous hostelry in the place; the *Gallo* was small and primitive. But we wanted to satisfy our own eyes. Coming to the *Gallo* by a back way, we did find it unpromising. A waiter, apron over arm, was in the door-way, and seeing us drive up, peer out, turn round and start away, came out to us invitingly. Our

leisurely procedure took several minutes, and in those minutes the
waiter was joined by the concierge, the portier, the little woman at
the desk, *due piccoli* and the grand proprietor himself. Pietro majestically continued his course, but to no avail. The waiter quickly
retired within and emerging at the entrance to the garage round the

FIGURE 77. ROOF-GARDEN AT THE MODERNO GALLO, BRESCIA

corner, headed us off. He renewed his entreaties — it was the best
hotel in the city — all the modern comforts — we had only to try it
to see. To Pietro's chagrin, we tried it, exceedingly to our advantage
and ultimately with his approval. He had not known that the
humble hostelry had been entirely made over and was now the *Albergo Moderno Gallo* — "Hotel Renovated Rooster." Near to our
clean and modern room on an upper floor was a pleasant little roof-
garden with a view of old house-tops and other attractions.

Across the street from our window was the *Duomo Nuovo*, begun in the seventeenth century, and next to it the *Duomo Vecchio* of the

FIGURE 78. *DUOMO NUOVO* AT BRESCIA

twelfth — a happy union of two different Classic styles long separated by the age of Gothic. Those saints on the gable of the façade

[89]

— we saw them standing out in glistening white against a sullen sky. For we had our first rain-fall at Brescia, preceded by a tramontana gale that swept the dust of the street as fiercely as that in Dante's Limbo. We watched it from the vestibule of the Broletto, a communal palace of the twelfth century, and when the *aer bruno* had

FIGURE 79. *DUOMO VECCHIO* AT BRESCIA

cleared and the smart shower was over, we strolled till dinner-time. Nothing attracted us more than the church of Santa Maria dei Miracoli, a little jewel of the Renaissance and a monument of Christian humanism (Figure 80). For while the sculptured pilaster at the right is inscribed with the very Christian injunction ERRORIS PAENITEAT, that on the left (blurred in our picture) bears the motto forever typical of Hellenism — μηδὲν ἄγαν, 'Nothing too much' (Figure 81).

Nor does Virgil fail to supply a motto in Brescia. A delightful

FIGURE 81. Μηδὲν ἄγαν ON THE CHURCH OF
SANTA MARIA DEI MIRACOLI AT BRESCIA

FIGURE 80. SANTA MARIA DEI MIRACOLI
AT BRESCIA

Renaissance house in the Via Porcellaga shows amidst the decorations on the façade the words

TRAHIT		SVA
QVEMQVE		VOLVPTAS

That is our motto for the present trip. One leaf of the double door is

FIGURE 82. MARKET AT BRESCIA

labelled INTROITVS; the other, with an admirable sense of completeness, ET EXITVS.

Next morning we lay in supplies for our way-side lunch. Market is in full flower and most of what we need can be purchased there. As we come away, someone else is also leaving, carting her purchases with her.

As we go to a *salumeria* for our bit of meat, we find that in Brescia only sausages may be procured in such an establishment; we must

FIGURE 83. HOME FROM THE MARKET AT BRESCIA

look up a *rosticceria*. That we discover in a picturesque cavern of a shop, which looks like a blacksmith's forge till you see what is going on. Over a blazing fire an oval spit is fastened to upright supports at

[93]

the right and the left of the hearth. The ends of the spit rest in sockets and it is turned — nowadays — by force of electricity. On the revolving rods of the spit, plump chickens are fastened and broil while they turn. Hot glows the work — *fervet opus* — and irresistible spreads the smell. We come away with one of those plump

FIGURE 84. ROMAN RUINS AT BRESCIA

chickens. When we put our teeth into it later, we fancied that it still was warm.

Our chief interest in Brescia is to see the two inscriptions that pin down Calvisano — or Carpenedolo? — as Virgil's birthplace. They are found in the *Museo Patrio d'Età Romana* appropriately established in the old Roman forum and including the picturesque remains of the Temple of Vespasian. We halt by a square pit containing tantalizing ruins and showing the level of the ancient city.

IN QUEST OF VIRGIL'S BIRTHPLACE

Before we enter the Museum, let us refresh our memory with the facts in the case, with gratitude to Professor Conway and his colleague Professor Braunholtz for their presentation of the evidence. One of the inscriptions that we are going to see — found at Calvisano — contains the name VERGILIA. To repeat Conway's statement once more,[58] there are only seven, or possibly eight other occurrences of the name *Vergilius* or *Vergilia* among the many thousand inscriptions from North Italy. Four come from districts outside the limits with which we are concerned and three are from Verona; the remaining one we will discuss in a moment. That the ninth was found at Calvisano and that Calvisano is thirty miles from Mantua is certainly a coincidence worth examining, in case the statement of Probus is to be taken exactly. But since Professor Conway would locate the farm at Carpenedolo, not at Calvisano, all that we can say of this inscription is that it was found at a spot about $4\frac{1}{2}$ English, or $4\frac{1}{5}$ Roman, miles away from "Andes," and that Probus's statement is not quite exact. Similarly with regard to the other inscription. This was found at neither Calvisano nor Carpenedolo but at Casalpoglio, about 8 English miles south of the latter town. This inscription contains the name of Publius Magius, a member of the family of Virgil's mother. Supposing that there is telling evidence for identifying the poet's birthplace with Carpenedolo, then one may say that not far from that place confirmatory evidence is found in the shape of these inscriptions. But these do not in themselves present a sufficient argument for locating the birthplace at Carpenedolo.

Let us note, incidentally, that the inscriptions containing the name of a member of the *gens Magia* are far more numerous than those with *Vergilius* or *Vergilia*. There are over forty in all, and these are distributed all over North Italy from Turin on the west to Aquileia on the east.[59] We may infer that Virgil's father married into a family more important than his own, exactly as Donatus, Virgil's commentator of the fourth century declares: "Some say that his father was a potter, but more say that he first was the hired man of a certain Magius, and later, as a reward for his industry, was given the hand of his daughter."[60] My point is that in view of the plentiful amount of Magian inscriptions and their wide dispersion in North Italian towns, the presence of one of them at Casalpoglio is not particularly striking evidence that the poet was born at a town eight miles away.

But it is time to stop theorizings and to cross the threshold of the Museum. Let the inscriptions speak for themselves. They are found in the central hall. Those that are not inscribed on altars or tombstones have been set into the walls, in the fashion familiar to visitors of the Galleria Lapidaria in the Vatican. It is an interesting display. The guide requests me to take no notes, but I have come provided with copies of the inscriptions that I wish to see, and memory retains enough to add notes upon them after we leave the Museum. Moreover, I am promised photographs of the inscriptions themselves.[61]

The little altar that bears the first inscription is considerably worn. Yes, as Conway noted, some of the lettering has crumbled away. It once read (there seems no doubt):

MATRONABVS
VERGILIA · C · F · VER(A)
PRO MVNATIA · T · F
CATVLLA · V · S · L · M

FIGURE 85. ALTAR ERECTED BY VERGILIA VERA (MUSEO ROMANO AT BRESCIA)
C. I. L. V 4137

Vergilia Vera erected this altar to the "Matrons," Celtic birth-deities, in behalf of Munatia Catulla (her daughter?) who was with child; the prayer was granted and the vow here duly paid. Catulla — dare we say that the households of two poets royal are united by this name?

The inscription on the other tomb (Figure 86) is better preserved.

```
        V                       F
     P · MAGIVS · MANI
     SIBI · ET · ASSELIAE · M · F
           SABINAE · VXORI
     ET · SATRIAE · M · F
           TERTIAE
     CASSIAE · P · F · SECVNDAE
           MATRI
```

This tomb, then, was erected in accordance with his vow by Publius Magius, son of Manius. It was to contain the remains of himself, his wife Assellia Sabina, his mother Cassia Secunda and a female relative Satria Tertia — a hospitable sepulchre.

Of prime importance, naturally, is the date of these inscriptions. Conway declares that the period to which they both belong is "Vergil's own," being "cut in the style which marked the best work between 50 B.C. and A.D. 50, but which from that epoch onwards, begins to be less usual." [62] They do not give quite this impression. Both inscriptions are in capital letters, but the style is not certainly that of the best work between 50 B.C. and A.D. 50. In the Virgilian inscription particularly, the character of the capitals verges on that which is called rustic.

We turn to the back wall of the Museum (Figure 87), where the *Inscriptiones Historicae* bespeak their dates; C. IVLIVS CAESAR —

[98]

FIGURE 86. TOMB OF P. MAGIUS MANIUS (MUSEO ROMANO AT BRESCIA)
C. I. L. V 4046

DRVSI ET GERMANICI — GERMANICO CAESARI — *there* is the grand style in Virgil's period and that which immediately succeeded. Of course it is true that ornamental square capital was not the only style cultivated during the Augustan age, whether the letters were written on papyrus or incised on stone. For a country altar one might not employ the lettering appropriate for a triumphal arch of state. But we have not enough material at our disposal — or if we have, it has not been studied with sufficient attention — to allow us to place these two inscriptions definitely within the years 50 B.C. — 50 A.D. Moreover the stately Augustan manner long prevailed. Look at the two inscriptions on the wall to the right and the left of that which bears the name of Germanicus Caesar. They are of the time of the Emperor Commodus of the third century of our era. They show capitals that are at least as good as those in our two inscriptions, which might conceivably have been incised as late as that. I do not believe that they were, particularly the Magian inscription, with its long I.[63] But even allowing for them both a date as early as the end of the first century B.C., that is not enough. If we wish to establish a birthplace by an inscription, the latter ought not to be much later than the date of the birth. That either of ours is as early as 70 B.C. is out of the question. Long before the date of his death in 19 B.C., Virgil had won a national reputation. His family, however humble when he was born, would have acquired a certain fame with him. Connections with other families outside little Andes might have been formed — possibly one with that of Catullus, for instance. That is all that we may safely infer from the altar erected by Vergilia Vera at Calvisano. And the evidence of the inscription of P. Magius is, as we saw, still less significant.

FIGURE 87. INSCRIPTIONS IN THE MUSEO ROMANO, BRESCIA

"But the most important point has still to be developed," I added. "Let's have it on the road," my patient listener replied, "for Pietro is probably anxious to get on." "Very well," said I, "but just let me ask one question first. If those inscriptions came from Mantuan towns, why were they appropriated by the Museum of

FIGURE 88. MONUMENT OF ARNOLD OF BRESCIA IN THE PIAZZA VENEZIA OF BRESCIA

Brescia? Why did we not see them at Mantua? Casalpoglio is at present in the *provincia Mantovana*. Was it not once in Brescia? And if so, did not Calvisano and Carpenedolo always belong to Brescia?" "Doubtless," she replied. "Come on."

Pietro might have waited a bit longer. We found him consuming a large and modern slice of the ancient *cucumis*. We got some of the fruit for ourselves in the Piazza Venezia, where the statue of Arnold of Brescia stands in his great revenge.

Being in the mood for inscriptions, I copy those on the base of the statue. In front, as a symbol of the new Italy of 1870 is inscribed:

AD · ARNALDO
AL · PRECVRSORE · AL · MARTIRE
DEL · LIBERO · ITALICO · PENSIERO
BRESCIA · SVA · DECRETAVA
TOSTO · INVENDICATA · IN · LIBERTA
DCCCCLXX

On the back is another Italian inscription. On the right is a quotation from an address made to the Emperor Frederick I by Roman envoys (LEGATI ROMANORUM AD REGEM) in 1155. It is taken from the German historian Otto of Freising,[64] and well represents the Roman republicanism of Arnold, apostle of free thought in the twelfth century.

REVERTANTVR · OPTO
PRISTINA · TEMPORA
ASSVREXI
AD · SACROSANCTVM
VRBIS · SENATVM
EQVESTREMQVE ORDINEM
INSTAVRANDVM
LEG · ROM · AD · REG ·
ANNO MCLV

In the inscription on the left, as fervid a Romanism is put into verse, with an appeal to the Gospel.[65]

IMPERIVM · TENEAT
ROMAE · SEDEAT · REGAT · ORBEM
PRINCEPS · TERRARVM
CAESARIS · ACCIPIAT
CAESAR · QVAE · SVNT
SVA · PRAESVL
VT · CHRISTVS · JVSSIT
GT · ROM · AD · REG ·
ANNO · MCXLIX

[103]

We now pass the barracks where Mussolini was a Bersagliere. "He never rose higher than sergeant then," said Pietro. But any buck-private knows that a sergeant can rule the world!

IX. BRESCIA TO VERONA

Out on the road again, retracing part of our course of yesterday. Castenedolo is passed. As we approach Montichiari a fine tower

FIGURE 89. THE RIVER CHIESE NEAR MONTICHIARI

looms in the distance. At the moment that we cross the Chiese it is entirely dry. No fault of the stream! Tityrus should not choose this occasion, however, for reposing *inter nota flumina*; he would gaze on nothing but a rocky road.

"Well, what about the inscriptions?" I am asked. Oh, yes. Why simply this. The most significant of them all was found and copied in the "greater church" at Pietole by the famous architect, antiquarian, epigraphist, palaeographer and general lover of learning, Fra Giocondo.[66] It runs:

P · VERGILIO · P · F
PONT · MAX
SABIN

The inscription no longer exists, and the *maior ecclesia* itself has passed away. Mommsen had thought the inscription a forgery, inspired by one that Ciriaco d'Ancona had seen by the river Tartaro near Verona, but Conway's defence of its genuineness seems to me impregnable.[67] Fra Giocondo at any rate was no forger, but a veracious and eminent man of wide learning,[68] whose testimony is here supported by Pacedianus, who copied the stone in 1517. The inscription as he found it is obviously a fragment, the meaning of which Conway has expounded. The latter would regard it as responsible for Dante's identification of Pietole with Andes.[69] I should hold not that Dante and the men of his time were prone to make archaeological deductions on the basis of inscriptions, as we are today, but rather that he accepted a tradition already current, and that it is for us, if we dare to believe the inscription genuine, to use it as evidence — not complete but corroborative evidence — of the tradition itself.

These things having been settled, we have eyes for the landscape again, and soon pass Montichiari, where the Brescian Alps stand out clearly in the background. Here is a flooded field, here one of rich red tilth, and here one thronged with soldiers occupied in maneuvres. We turn off at the left from a dark avenue of cypresses leading to a

FIGURE 90. AVENUE OF CYPRESSES NEAR MONTICHIARI

private estate, like that which we had imagined had once conducted guests to *La Virgiliana* in the days of the Gonzaga.

We enter the *provincia* of Mantua again at its northwestern tip. As we make a turn at Castiglione, a mountain outlines the end of the road. This is picturesque country. Moreover, there is a ridge, nearly if not quite, as imposing as that at Carpenedolo. At one point on it is a church, with a cemetery guarded by cypresses. This is the point where runs the stream noted by Professor Conway on Kiepert's map but not found by him in May 1923.[70] It is, today, the Fluvio Osone,

FIGURE 91. RIDGE AT CASTIGLIONE

which enters into the Lago Superiore of the Mincio; and I am not sure that we saw it either. My notes do make mention of a very fine concrete canal which may have momentarily diverted the waters of the Osone in May 1923 and August 1929. The stream in its natural condition would suffice for Tityrus, and so would its affiliated canals.

So, then, here is his farm at last — in the *provincia Mantovana.* Ah, but it is only some 21 Roman miles away from the city! Still, Carpenedolo is not over 25. But no inscription was found here! Still, none was found at Carpenedolo.

Two tired shepherds (or rather laborers on the road) are taking their siesta by the canal. We are reminded that it is time for luncheon and turn down a little road where we find a spot under the trees. The *pollo* that we saw broiled with our own eyes soon disappears forever, and we take to the road again. Certain vestiges of the War

FIGURE 92. VOLTA MANTOVANA

are noticeable, such as a barn turned into a depot of ammunition — grenades and shells. Here is barbed wire, used not to ward off the foe but to prevent pacificists from exploding the ammunition — not all Italians were one for the cause in those troublous days. We reach Guidozzolo. All along the route we see how mountains "sink into the plain." Volta Mantovana comes, with an impressive tower, of which I take a too distant view as we look back at it.

FIGURE 83. RIDGE NEAR VALEGGIO

FIGURE 94. HILLS AT VALEGGIO

We have mounted from 63 metres at Guidozzolo to 103 at Volta, and now descend towards the valley of the Mincio. We follow a blind trail to the undiscoverable Bussachetti, then back to a turn of the road and a villa named *Prima Vera*, where men are having a game of

FIGURE 95. THE MINCIO AT VALEGGIO

nine-pins. We pass a donkey-cart and various rocky fields. The hills on either side of us are brown and bleak. Canals are dry — but ah, here is a pretty vista of fertile fields and their boundaries of mulberry trees and, on beyond, a pleasant ridge (Figure 93). We have passed into the province of Verona, descend to the Mincio, and cross it at Valeggio. Here at last is worthy scenery for Virgil's farm. Lovely hills lie all about us (Figure 94). At many a spot one could locate a small estate, sloping from a hill to the river. The Mincio is at its best, partly with the aid of an old tower. An artist is painting it, while a little group of admirers, including two priests, is watching his work proceed.

We have been looking up stream from the left end of the bridge. Even better is the view from the right end which displays a little

FIGURE 96. THE MINCIO AT VALEGGIO

water-fall. Nor is the view of the bridge itself with a crenellated tower and a campanile in the distance without its charm (Figure 97).

The little place is dirty, as full of miscellaneous rubbish as the streets of lower New York, but we want some memento of it. One more expert than I steps into the shop of Adelelmo Benaglia, proprietor of a *rameria*, and comes back with a copper kettle. The hospitable little woman in the shop, going to the extreme of courtesy, will allow the Signora to adopt her pretty little daughter, who thus will see America the Great and send back word about a cousin, gone to "San Paolo" three years ago, though not a word from him since. Our luggage is already ample, and the offer must be reluctantly declined. While these negotiations are in progress, I take a view of a house with a little mill (Figure 98).

I stroll about for other views, but though many might be taken, perhaps I have enough. This is the spot of spots. It is with a real

FIGURE 97. BRIDGE OVER THE MINCIO AT VALEGGIO

intuition that Sir William Ramsay chose a site for Virgil's farm on the west bank of the Mincio opposite Valeggio.[71] To be sure, Valeggio is only some 15 miles from Mantua — we *are* getting away from Probus. Moreover, Professor Conway has raised some telling objections against Ramsay's view, in case we try to fit all the details described in the *Eclogues* into the scenery displayed to us at Valeggio.[72] Well, then, *no* site that we have examined will quite do, for the reason that Virgil's imagination takes bits of them all and surpasses them all. And yet I would not deny that Moeris's description of the land saved by the master's song means something definite.

Back to Servius! And through him to Donatus, and to commentators from whom the latter drew. We find a welter of explanations, as usual, but among them is one clear tradition that Conway does not

FIGURE 98. HOUSE AT VALEGGIO

cite. It is that the land won back by the poet's songs was not merely his own little farm — though the commentators give that explanation, too, — but all that Mantua had lost.[73] The commentators also relate that Octavius Musa, appointed surveyor by Augustus in the disputes about boundaries, avenged a private grudge against the Mantuans by measuring off 15 miles of Mantuan territory and handing it over to Cremona.[74] We are also told that Alfenus Varus, who had received a like commission, was ordered to leave to Mantua three miles round the city from its wall, but actually allowed it scarce 800 paces ($\frac{4}{5}$ of a Roman mile) — i. e., nothing but its marshes.[75]

The purchaser comes out of the copper-shop triumphant. Look at this map, I exclaim, after explaining my cogitations.[76] Put the edge of this paper on a direct line connecting Cremona and Mantua. The boundary line between the two *provincie* here coincides with the River Oglio, just west of Canneto, which we should have visited the other day were it not for that happy detour. Now the modern boundary is exceedingly serpentine at this point. It follows the Oglio only to make a loop towards the south, adding two other loops before it completes its southern course. An exact calculation were unprofitable, since we do not know exactly where the ancient boundary ran. But if we take as an average a point on the first loop half-way between the River Oglio on the west and the end of the loop on the east, and suppose that at that point Octavius Musa started out with his ten-foot pole to measure off 15 Roman miles, or 22.4 kilometres, we shall mark the end of 15 miles at a point just a bit to the east of Curtatone, which we passed on the way from Mantua to Le Grazie, little realizing its importance at the time. Now lay on the yard-stick again. From this point to the outskirts of the city it is just about 4.5 kilometres or 3 Roman miles. That is what was left after Octavius Musa got through, and that is what Varus was told to allow the Mantuans, but the villain cut them down to the marshes. These two statements of the commentators, then, neatly dovetail together, provided the ancient boundary was practically what the modern one is. Or is all this mere chance?

"Hardly," was the courteous reply. Well, then, Mantua had lost all its land except its marshes and, before Varus, the three-mile ring round the city. Virgil's farm at Andes was 3 miles away, and might just have been saved, or just have been gobbled up, or first saved and then gobbled up; it was on the firing-line. But Virgil is more concerned about his city than about his farm. If you want to describe, in poetry, what Mantua lost, and what the songs of the master won back for a time, you can begin at the north, where the hills melt into the plain, as they have done for us all along our route today, and come down to the water, the lagoons of the Mincio, that is, and the beech grove somewhere near the city. That is what Virgil meant.

"Q. E. D." said she. More than that, I added, it is plain why Virgil wrote this particular eclogue, the *Ninth*, with a hint to Varus in it, and why — a bit later, I imagine — he apportioned part of the honor of the *Sixth Eclogue* to him. He may not have got much out of him, but the *First Eclogue*, distinctly not the first in order of composition, shows that something was obtained from Virgil's new hero, the god-like Octavian. At least somebody in that eclogue obtained something — and somebody didn't.

"Doesn't the poet bring in Mantua again in the *Georgics*?" A good point, I rejoin. He is speaking of soil that is especially fertile.

> Like the rich fields which hapless Mantua lost,
> Whose reed-fringed river pastures snow-white swans,
> Where clear springs ne'er shall fail the flocks,
> Nor meadow-grass; for what the cattle crop
> All the long day, the cooling dew restores
> In the short night.[77]

"You quoted that before on the way from Milan." Yes, but I didn't see all its meaning then. It means, I rather think now, that even the *First Eclogue*, though it may have preserved the family farm for Virgil's father, did not win back what the town as a whole had

FIGURE 99. RUINS NEAR VALEGGIO

lost. In any case, it is clear that Virgil is talking of all Mantua here and not his farm.[78] Our modest poet would hardly identify the city with himself. And in these lines he has in mind the Mincio with its reedy swamp by Pietole and its swans, I suppose, anywhere in its stream. He also has in mind the clear springs of the northern hills and the glad fields that we have seen everywhere.[79]

"Excellent. *En voiture.*"

After this exertion, I am glad to take things easy as we accomplish the final stretch to Verona. Some ruins near Valeggio attract us.

We pass rocky fields and the new canals that will recreate them. Now comes a modern watering-cart, and now men are getting water from the canal with a long-handled scoop and throwing it on the road. That darling of Vesta, the donkey, of whom Virgil's *Copa* sings, is

FIGURE 100. DONKEY CART NEAR VALEGGIO

still to be seen. The mountains on the left become more and more lovely as we approach Verona. We enter, and make for our hotel. Having had experience with bird-hotels, and birds of gold, we make for the *Colomba d'Oro*. Alas, its chambers are full, and we content ourselves with the *Londra*.

X. VERONA

Next morning we are confronted with a problem. Verona is our journey's end with Pietro, and he is booked to return at once. Of course he might take us with him as far as Desenzano, but then there are inscriptions, both Virgilian and Magian, to inspect. And Verona

FIGURE 101. SAN ZENO AT VERONA

itself could repay the traveller for many days. We had seen a bit, with Diana's help, after our arrival. We made first for San Zeno, one of the wonders of architecture. Begun in the twelfth century and finished in the fourteenth, it has suffered few alterations, down to the present day. Only a little of its charm is shown by our views of the portal and of the exquisitely simple cloisters (Figure 102).

Fully as impressive is the crypt, partly built of ancient Roman

FIGURE 102. THE CLOISTERS OF SAN ZENO, VERONA

FIGURE 103. FROM THE PONTE PIETRA AT VERONA

columns and marble beams. We emerge with the deep sense of antiquity, of the Pagan foundation of Christian culture that often awes the traveller in Rome. We look about again at this ancient basilica, filled at the moment with the organ music of Bach. We ascend to the choir, and there at the organ is a young priest, as in

FIGURE 104. ROMAN THEATRE AT VERONA

Giorgione's picture; two boys sit by him, all eyes, and all ears, in rapt admiration of their master.

Diana takes us quickly to the other end of the city, across the Ponte Pietra, with a view of old houses and the Romanesque church of Santo Stefano (Figure 103).

We are on our way to the remains of the Roman theatre, a work of the Augustan age, as yet only incompletely excavated. In the above view is shown the entrance to the *cavea* or auditorium, at the right. The seats in the *cavea* are visible at the left and are plainer still in the picture that follows. That the outer wall of the stage-

FIGURE 105. ROMAN THEATRE AT VERONA

buildings was faced with marble is shown by the sockets in the wall. An arcade adjoined it, of which columns remain. Time has stripped off part of their marble facing from the core of brick. There they stand, like noblemen with frayed doublets, monuments of shabby gentility.

We had done enough to deserve our dinner. After it we had a frappé, a specialty of a café in the Piazza Erbe, once the forum of Roman days, and still true to the ancient outlines. The frappé was

FIGURE 106. ROMAN THEATRE AT VERONA

not good. It suggested the dregs of an American ice cream soda and prompted further wanderings. The night was mysterious and black, but the flickering city lights gave the outlines of the old favorites that we wanted to see again — the Piazza dei Signori and its Loggia — the tombs of the Scaligeri. Modern ugliness sank into the shadows. Ancient beauty concealed in the dark the ravages of time and stood forth in youthful freshness. This is the way to know the Verona of Shakespeare and of romance.

IN QUEST OF VIRGIL'S BIRTHPLACE

XI. VERONA TO DESENZANO

Morning came and we made our decision. We had seen Verona at its best and would not spoil the vision. Why pother about the inscriptions? It would take at least a day to hunt them all, and we had studied the most important ones at Brescia. Moreover, we now could go with Pietro. That was our real reason, well buttressed with ostensibilities. So to the road on a heavenly day, with shimmering lights on the mountains.

"Yes, but after all, how about Probus? Aren't you still worried a little about those 30 miles?" I know it, my dear. Let's think about it on the way. The commentary that has come down under the name of the great scholar of the first century is admittedly not the original work, though it may contain extracts from it. Admittedly also, the prefatory life of Virgil contains excellent matter and has none of the obvious legends conspicuous in the account that Donatus drew from Suetonius. If Probus says that Andes was 30 miles from Mantua, we should submit that statement to a respectful examination. And first, we should inspect the genuineness of the text — *rustico vico Andico, qui abest a Mantua milia passuum* XXX. Conway, with his usual thoroughness, has discussed the matter.[80] The three manuscripts known to editors — one at Paris, one at Munich, one at Rome, unite in reading XXX, and with them agrees the edition of Virgil which appeared at Rome in 1471, and which for the work of Probus is the *editio princeps*.[81] To be sure, Egnatius in his edition, Venice, 1507, reads not XXX but III; he professes, further, to have based his text on a *codex vetustissimus* from the monastery of Bobbio, but this manuscript cannot be found today.[82]

Enthusiastic humanists of the Renaissance were not always precise in their evaluation of the manuscripts that lent strength to their new editions of a Classical work,[83] so that without actually calling Egnatius a liar in our haste we should likewise not in our haste be sure that a very ancient codex was accessible to him. Conway puts the matter thus:[84]

"In any case, no scholar with any critical experience can hesitate as to which of the readings is more likely to be right, the XXX (of four known witnesses) or the III (of the one, now lost); for no mediaeval scribe would think of changing III to XXX in such a statement; whereas only too many of them were likely to take the easy way out of the difficulty, which has been taken even by some modern editors, who ought to know better, and who have calmly tried to abolish the evidence which their ignorance of ancient Italy . . . made them unable to understand."

This is a clear and vigorous statement of that principle of textual criticism, first definitely enunciated by the great Bentley, whereby the more difficult of two readings, the *lectio difficilior*, should be preferred to the easier. For the more difficult reading is just the kind that a scribe, or a reviser, would tend to make easier, whereas the easier reading would be left as it is.

"Well, then, doesn't that settle this text?" No, I reply, I think not, at least not without further discussion. The principle of the *lectio difficilior*, while a good working rule, is by no means an absolute criterion. The false application of it has sometimes worked havoc with texts. In the present case —

But how can we talk of the criticism of texts with the glory of Lake Garda at last before us? There are indescribable colors on the

FIGURE 107. LAKE GARDA

FIGURE 108. THE RIVER MINCIO AT LAKE GARDA

water, white caps on the waves, and real surf breaking on the beach (Figure 107). So Virgil told the truth in his surging verse—

fluctibus et fremitu assurgens Benace marino.[85]

When a storm sweeps Lake Garda, its waves may well rival those of the sea. Either bank is visible from the other side, and yet in this, the lower end of the lake, the breadth is of no mean extent.

FIGURE 109. THE RIVER MINCIO AT LAKE GARDA

We are at Pescheria, hard by the Albergo Virgilio. It is here that the Mincio starts the pleasant course that we have seen at several points. Two outlets, which are pictured in the preceding views, unite below in the splendid stream, up which Catullus once upon a time, may (or may not) have come in a sailboat to Sirmio.

IN QUEST OF VIRGIL'S BIRTHPLACE

We are to sail, or steam, after him, proceeding from Desenzano, whence Tennyson once went out in a rowboat. The landscape is not particularly "olive-silvery"; in fact we have noticed few if any olive trees on the way. In the town we behold what seems a miracle, or at least a contradiction in terms, a motor bus attached to a trolley above but to no rails below. Our boat leaves at 10.15 and it is only 9.20 now. We can bid Pietro a long and tearful good-bye and leave at least a half-hour for textual criticism. But what is this? Crowds on the gang-plank? We are in time, if we move briskly, for an earlier and unexpected boat, provided for the Sunday crowd. We make our adieux in short order — perhaps this is easier after all — and secure the last seats on deck. Pietro and Diana are scouring the plain towards Milan.

XII. LAKE GARDA

No textual criticism till Sirmio is passed, and only between stops while we cease to exclaim at the wild beauties of Lake Garda. Catullus's all-but-island comes into view with the surf breaking at its tip, and — yes — plenty of olive trees on the shore (Figure 110).

The landing is by Albergo Eden — there is also an Albergo Catullo of course — and with the incoming crowd is a band that blows us entertainment as far as Gardone (Figure 111).

Now then to our muttons — and to their parchments on which the commentary of Probus is preserved. How venerable is the antiquity of the four witnesses to the text that offset the evidence of Egnatius? One is the *editio princeps*, no manuscript at all. It was based on some manuscript, but what that was no mortal knows. We can reach back no earlier than 1471, the date of the edition. Now take a glance at these photographs, procured through the courtesy of my friends at Paris, Munich and Rome.[86] (We inspect our treasures discreetly, and no crowd forms.) First, the Paris manuscript. This book is written in what is called the humanistic cursive script of the fifteenth century. One may not define its date too nicely, but it

FIGURE 110. SIRMIO

might well be that it is no older than the *editio princeps* — perhaps not quite so old (Figure 112).

Very similar is the appearance of the Vatican manuscript. Here again we have the humanistic script of a legible variety. The exact date is no easier to determine than that of the Bibliothèque Nationale (Figure 113).

The remaining manuscript is from Munich (Figure 114). It gives us a certain thrill because the name of the writer is well known —

he is Petrus Crinitus, the famous humanist. We also know just when he made the present copy; it was on October 6, 1496, twenty-five years after the *editio princeps* of Probus's commentary appeared.[87] Like some other scholars he writes an abominable hand—not so illegible when you are used to it — one even gets fond of the eccentricities

FIGURE 111. WHARF AT SIRMIO

like the use of the Greek ϕ for *ph* — but at first glance it seems hopeless. Even the great Mommsen found it "schwer zu lesen." "Yes, just like your love-letters, which I used to leave round with impunity after one of my friends thought that they were written in German script."

For a happy contrast, look at the beautiful Roman type in which Egnatius set his edition of Virgil's works in 1507 (Figure 115). He includes in this edition of Virgil the commentary of Servius and like-

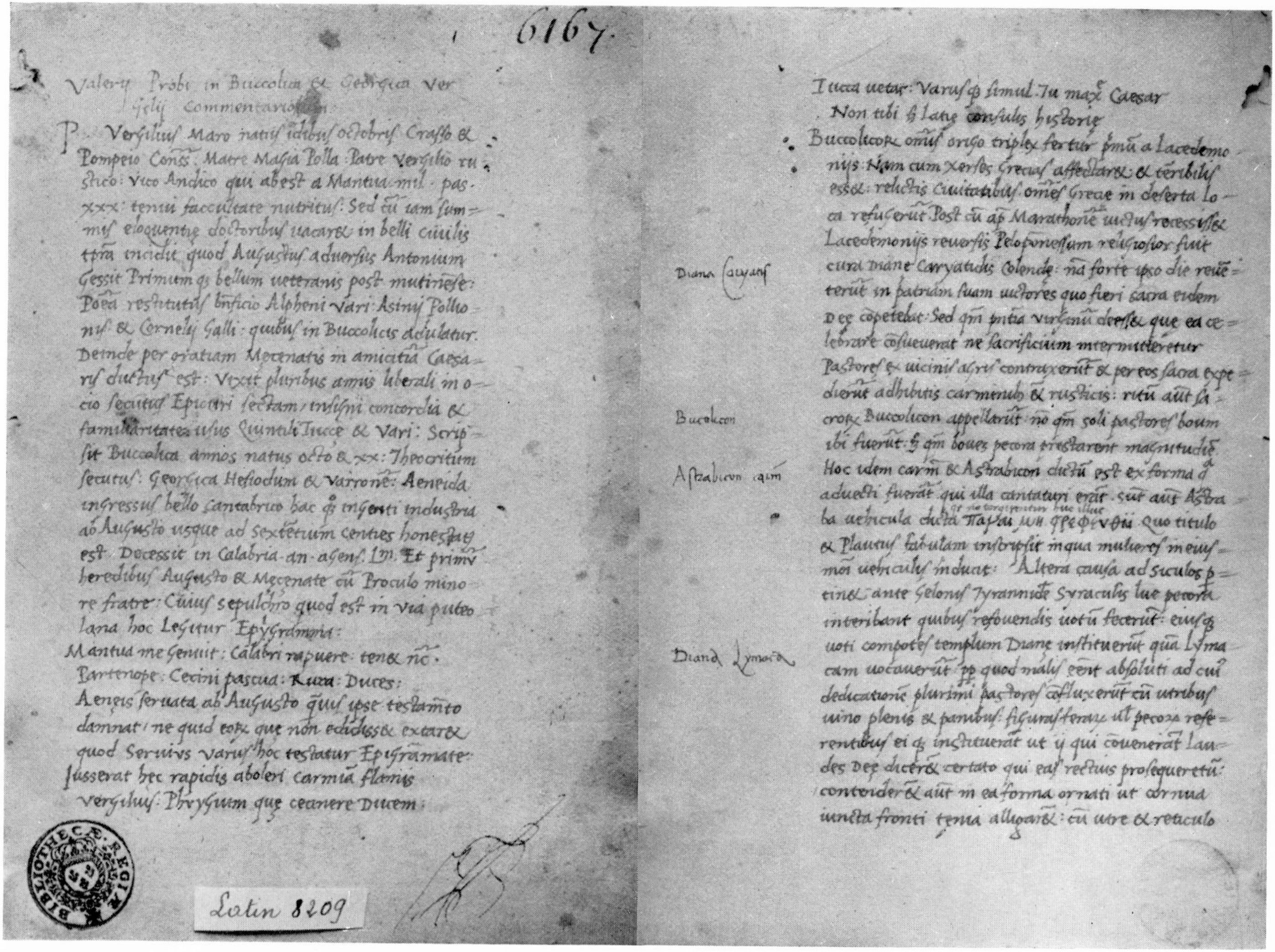

FIGURE 112. *CODEX PARISINUS B. N. LAT.* 8209, FOLL. 1r AND 1v

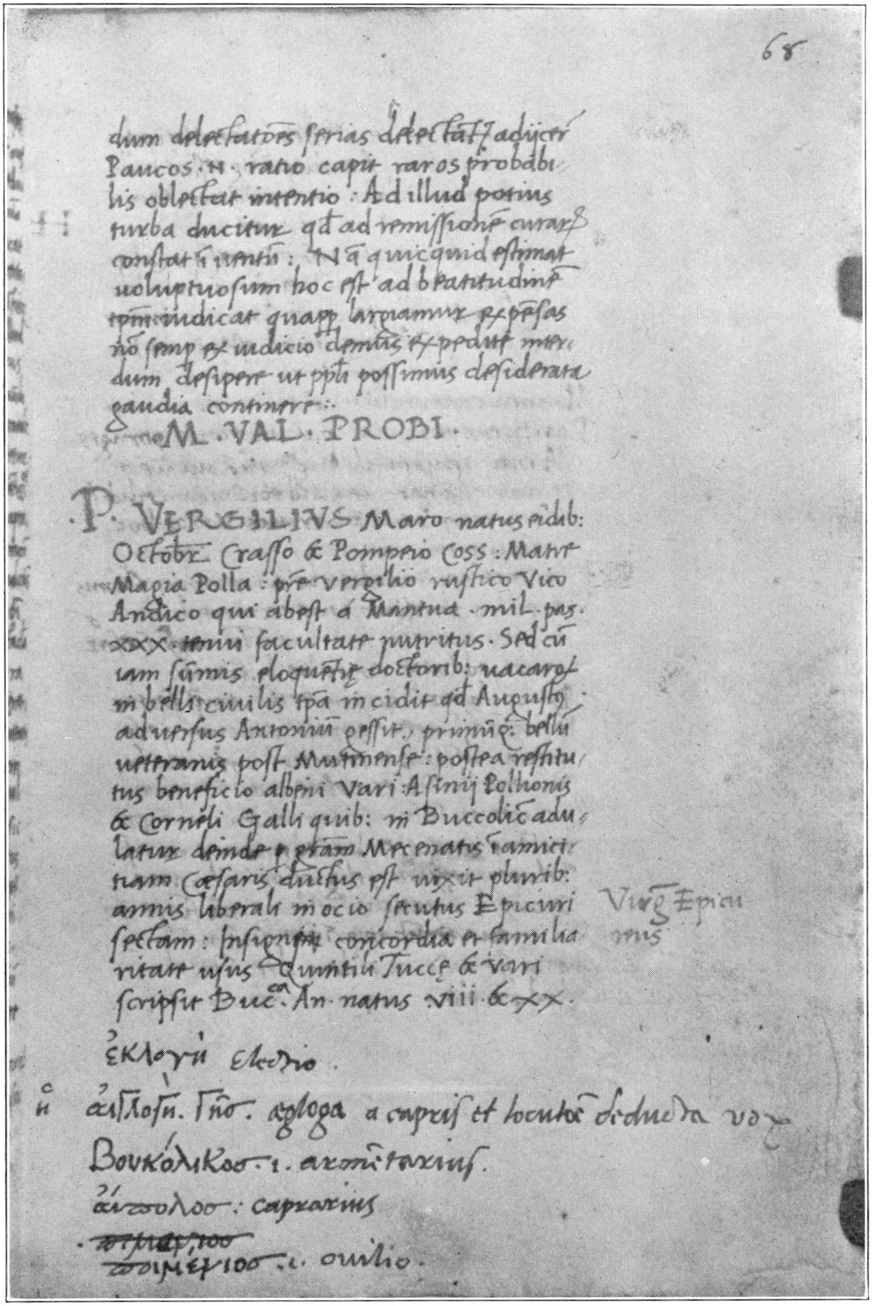
dum delectatores serias delectat adiicere
Paucos .n. raro capit raros probabi
lis oblectat intentio: Ad illud potius
turba ducitur qd ad remissionem curarum
constat inventum: Nam quicquid estimat
voluptuosum hoc est ad beatitudinem
tpm indicat quapropter largiamur ex pessas
no semper ex iudicio demus ex probant inter
dum desipere ut ppti possimus desiderata
gaudia continere:.
M. VAL. PROBI.
P. VERGILIUS Maro natus idib:
Octobr. Crasso & Pompeio coss: Matre
Magia Polla: patre Vergilio rustico Vico
Andico qui abest a Mantua mil. pas.
XXX. tenui facultate nutritus. Sed cum
iam summis eloquentie doctorib: vacaret
in belli civilis tpa incidit qd Augustus
adversus Antonium gessit, primumque bellum
veteranis post Mutinense: postea restitu
tus beneficio alpheni Vari: Asinii Pollionis
& Cornelii Galli quib: in Buccolicis adu
latur deinde per gratiam Mecenatis in amici
tiam Cesaris ductus est vixit plurib:
annis liberali in ocio secutus Epicuri
sectam: insigni concordia et familia
ritate usus Quintilii Tucce & Vari
scripsit Bucca. An. natus viii & xx.
Virg Epicu reus
ἐκλογη electio
... egloga a capris et locutione ...
Βουκολικος .i. armentarius
αἰπολος: caprarius
ποιμενικος .i. ovilio

FIGURE 113. *CODEX VATICANUS LAT.* 2930, FOL. 68ʳ

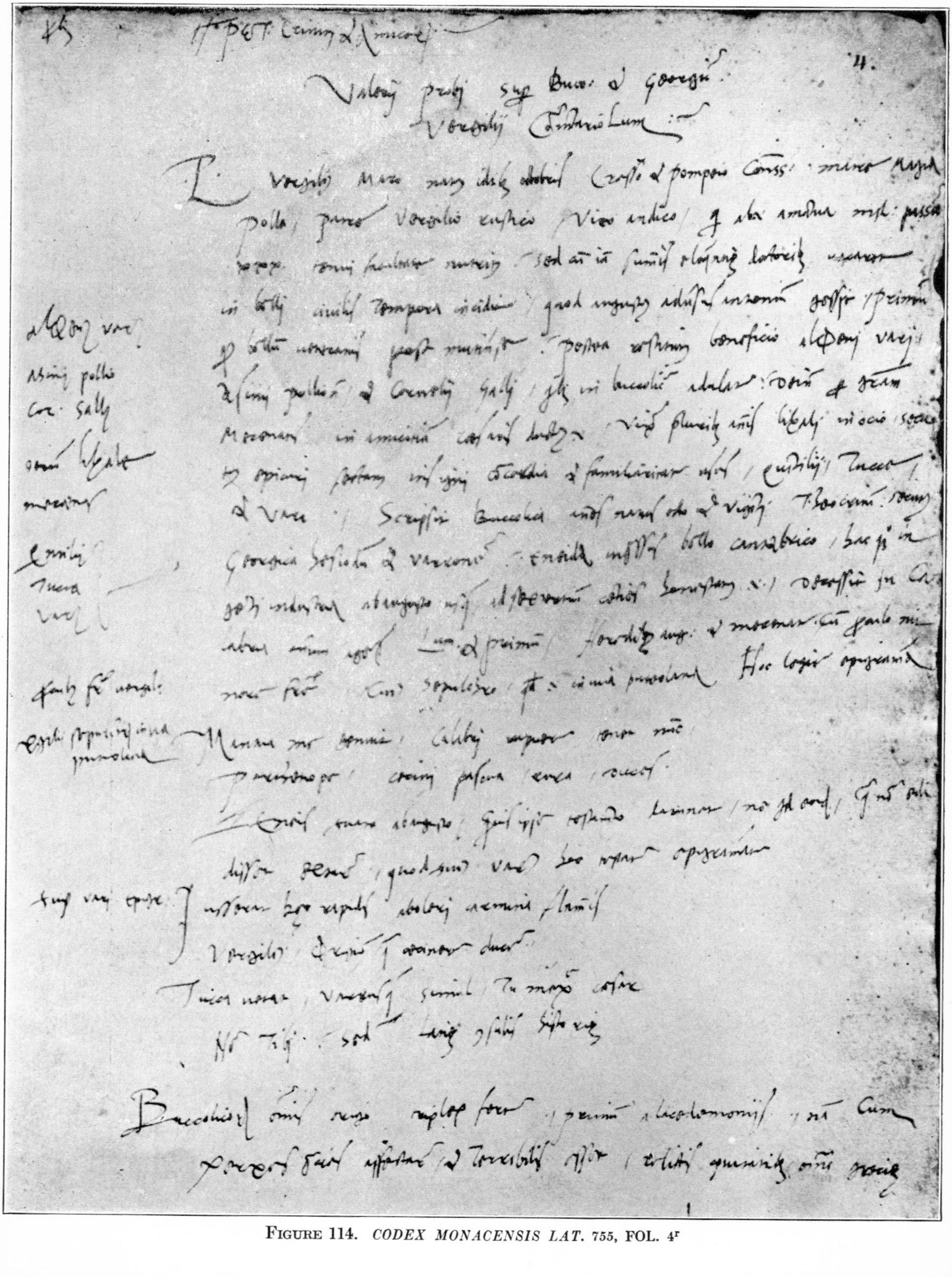

FIGURE 114. *CODEX MONACENSIS LAT.* 755, FOL. 4[r]

VBLIVS VIRGILIVS MARO NATVS IDIBVS OCTOBRIBVS
Craſſo τ Pompeio cōſſ. Matre Magia Polla:Patre Virgilio ruſtico: Vico andi
co:qui abeſt à Mantua millia paſſuum.iij.tenui facultate nutritus.Sed quum iſ
ſummis eloquentiæ doctoribus vacaret:in belli ciuilis tempora incidit: quod
Auguſtus aduerſus Antonium geſſit primumqʒ.

Poſt mutinenſe bellum veteranis.

¶POSTEA reſtitut°bñficio Alpheni Varri Aſinij Pollionis τ Cornelij Galli:qbus in bucoli
cis adulatur. Deinde per gratiam Mœcenatis ı amicitiam Cæſaris ductus eſt: vixit pluri
bus. In ocio ſecutus Epicuri ſectam · inſigni con
cordia τ familiaritate vſus Quintilij:Tuccæ:τ Varri.Scripſit bucolica annos natus octo τ
xx.Theocritus ſecutus:Georgica Heſiodum et Varronem: Aeneida ingreſſus bello cantabri
co:Hoc quoqʒ ingenti induſtria:ab Auguſto vſqʒ ad ſeſtertium centies honeſtatus eſt. Deceſ
ſit in Calabria annum agens quinquageſimuʒ primum:Hæredibus Auguſto τ Mœcænate
cũ Proculo minore Fratre:quoius ſepulchro:qd eſt in via puteolana hoc legit Epigramma?

Mantua me genuit. Calabri rapuere.tenet nunc
Parthenope.cecini paſcua:rura:duces.

¶ÆNEIS ſeruata eſt ab Auguſto quãuis ipſe teſtamento cauiſſet:ne quid eorum quæ non
ædidiſſet:extaret:Quod Seruius Varrus hoc teſtatur Epigrammate?

Iuſſerat hæc rapidis aboleri carmina flammis
Virgilius:phrygium quæ cecinere ducem.
Tucca vetat:Varruſqʒ ſimul:tu maxime cæſar
Non ſinis.ſed latiæ conſulis hiſtoriæ.

¶BVCOLICORV M omnis origo triplex eſſe fertur primum a Lacedæmonijs.Nã quus
Xerxes græcias affectaret:τ terribilis eſſet:relictis ciuitatibus omnis græcia gens in deſerta
loca refugerunt.Poſt quum apud Marathonē victus receſſiſſe:lacedæmonijs reuerſis in Pelo
ponneſu:religioſior fuit cura Dianæ Caryatidis colendæ.Nam forte ipſo die reuerterunt in
patriã victores:quo fieri ſacra eidem deæ cõpetebat.Sed quoniã præſentia virginuʒ deeſſet:
quæ ea celebrare cõſueuerãt:ne ſacrificium intermitteretur:paſtores ex vicinis agris contra
Xerunt:τ per eos ſacra expedierunt adhibitis carminibus etiã ruſticis:Rītũ aũt ſacrorũ bu
colicon appellarũt. Non quoniã ſolũ boum paſtores ibi fuerũt:ſed qñ boues pecora præſta
rent magnitudine.Hoc idẽ carmen Aſtrabicõ dictũ eſt a forma ſedilis qua aduecti fuerant.
qui illa cantãturi erant. Sunt autem aſtraba vehicula dicta παρὰ τὸ μὴ ϛρέφεϲϑαι : quo
titulo τ Plautus fabulam inſcripſit:In qua mulieres in eiuſmodi vehiculis inductæ. Altera
cauſa ad ſiculos pertinet.Ante Gelonis tyrannideʒ Syracuſis lue pecora interibãt:Quibus
refouendis votum fecerunt.eiuſqʒ voti compotes templum Dianæ inſtituerunt:quam Lya
cam vocauerunt:propter quod malis eſſent abſoluti:ad eius dedicationeʒ plurimi paſtores
confluxerunt cum vtribus vino plenis:τ panibus figuras ferarum vel pecorum referenti
bus:eiqʒ inſtituerunt vt qui conuenerant Laudes deæ decãtarēt certato qui eas rectius proſe
queretur:contenderet autem in ea forma ornati:vt cornua fronti adiuncta tænia obligarē
cum vtre:τ reticulo:quo panificia haberent cum claua: eum qui viciſſet:præmium haberet:
qd is qui victus erat:contuliſſet: permiſſumqʒ vt inde irent:τ quibus cantauerant:eiſdem
illis fauſta ominarentur:quod genus religionis hodie conuerſum eſt in queſtum:Idem ſunt
enim:qui bucoliſtæ nominantur. Tertia opinio ad eoſdem Siculos pertinet:Sed ex alia ra
tione. Nam Oreſtes poſt paricidium furens reſponſo didicit qd deponeret furorem ita de
muʒ:Si recupata Sorore Iphigenia ablueretur fluuio:quod ſeptem fluminibus confunderet:
diu vexatus:quuʒ in taurica Iphigeniã reperiſſet:venit ad fines Rheginoruʒ. Ibiqʒ inuento
flumine elutus traiecit in Siciliaʒ:τ iuxta Syracuſas ſomnio admonitus ſimulacrũ deæ:
qd ſecus de Taurice aduexerat templo poſito cõſecrauit:quas appellauit Faſcelitim. Siuedʒ
faſce lignoruʒ tectum de Taurice ſimulacrũ extuliſſet. Eius deæ nomen breui adprobatã:
propter quod plurima pecora muneri quiſqʒ; conferebat:Quæ quum incrementaſſent:non
defuerunt qui gratuitam cuſtodiendis operam adhiberent contenti tanqʒ conſtitutã merce
dem lactis vel caſei Huius autẽ fluminis:apud quod purgatus eſt.Oreſtes. Varro meminit
humanarum.x.ſic:iuxta Rheginuʒ fluuij ſunt cõtinui ſeptem latapadon:migodes: eurgyon:
ſtacteros: polme:melciſſa:argeades. In his e matris nece dicitur purgatus Oreſtes . Ibiqʒ
diu fuiſſe enſem:τ ab eo ædificatus Apollinis templus quoius loco Rheginos quũ delphos
proficiſcerentur re diuina facta Lauream decerpere ſolitos:quam ferrent ſecum. Item Ca
to in originibus tertio: Rhegini taurocini vocantur.de fluuio:qui præterfluit.Id oppidum
arunci primo poſſederunt. Idẽ achæi troia domum redeuntes in eorum agro fluuij ſunt ſex

FIGURE 115. PUBLII VIRGILII BUCOLICA, GEORGICA, AENEIS, ED. IO. BAPTISTA
EGNATIUS, VENETIIS, 1507, FOL. A VIII R.

aut p̃o Seruio agnofci, aut agnitus, p̃cipi fatis poffet· Verũ in nulla ei⁹ opis
pte grauius ꝺefæuitũ erat, q̃ vbi homericos verfus ad cui⁰ filũ Maro p̃cipue
carmen fuu₃ texuerat, citaffet· Quare cũ pené infinita quæ ꝺeerant adden⧸
da ex fcriptis manu codicibus cenfuiffem, Sexcentos p̃ærerea ⱬ amplius cu₃
Homeri tum alio̱ in poffeffioné legitimam verfus vendicantes· Dimidiatu₃
Seruium atq₃ ideo fœdum, integru₃ (vt opino̱) et nitidu₃ fecimus·interim tñ
id temperamentũ adhibuimus, vt quædam, quod ad Geographiam attinet,
immutare noluerim. In reliquis adeo elabo̱atu₃ a nobis eft, vt fi tres aut ad
fummum quatuo̱ ꝺemas locos; omnia tibi iam perfpicua ⱬ aperta effe pof⧸
fint. His P̃obi commétariolus in Bucólica ⱬ Geó̱gica, tametfi ꝺecurtatus,
ⱬ ipfe nec fatis integer accedet· Cuius tibi lectio non paru₃ voluptatis (vt fpe⧸
ro) nouitate fua, ⱬ vtilitatis eruditione allatura fit. Cæterũ ꝺe his melius qui
legent· illud c̃p in Maroniani carminis emendatione fecuti fumus, Diligen⧸
tem lecto̱é admonitu₃ p̃cipue velim· Nos in eo emendando, multa ad vetu⸱
ftæ ꝑfuetudinis no̱má, Cuius Vergiliũ obferuantiffimum fuiffe conftat, ꝺi
rexiffe· in plerifq₃ antiq̱oribus potius aucto̱ibus q̃ recétib⁰ grámaticis ad⧸
ftipulatos· In alijs no v̄fq₃ adéo ad viuu₃ refecuiffe, vt aliqd vulgatæ cuidá
ꝑfuetudini noluerim ꝺatu₃·q̃n parce quoq₃ nec femp éadem in eifdé aufus
fum, ne ferulas licentioru₃ grámatico̱ tanq̃ craḇonum Aculeos irritarem·
vt fiquid vetuftatis inerit, ad vetuftio̱es ꝓuocatio itegra fit·fiqd rurfus no
uitatem redolebit; hofce Criticos placatio̱es habeam . Hæc igitur tibi oĩa,
immenfu₃ fane opus ⱬ infinitas pené vigilias meæ erga patré tuum Clariffi⧸
mũ, ⱬ Optimu₃ virũ beniuolentiæ teftes fempiternos, neq; no in te iuuene₃
non nobiliffimũ folum oium ⱬ familiæ vetuftate, ⱬ a maio̱ibus tuis re̱
geftaru₃ amplitudine, fed fummæ Indolis ⱬ fpectatiffimæ p̱obitatis,
Hæc inq̃ tibi oĩa ⱬ ꝺico ⱬ nuncupo· Tum vt q ex viua noftra vo⧸
ce induftria₃ ꝓbafti p̃æfens, Abfens quoq₃ eius aliquez fructũ
capias · Tum vt nos eo effe in te animo intelligas , vt nihil
antiqus q̃ me vobis oibus ho̱is·omni loco , omni tpe q̃
chariffimũ eé, habeá. Ea eft p̃terea poetæ huius lectio,
quæ no te folum literarũ cupidiffimum, ve̱ etiam
quéuis aliũ ⱬ ꝺelectare et iuuare plurimũ poffit,
in qua fi vt ꝺebes verfabere, No ꝺiffido quin
ad fummá familiæ tuæ Nobilitaté, Maxi
mu₃ hoc quoq₃ literarium Decus acce⧸
dat. Quod ⱬ patris imitatione vel re⧸
centi epiftolarum editione Ce⧸
lebris , et noftra adho̱tatio⧸
ne facere ꝺebes·Cum p̱æ⧸
fertim hac ætate in quo
aut tutius, aut hone
ftius te exerceas
q̃ in Literis ni⧸
hil habeas.
VALE.
✠

FIGURE 116. VIRGIL, ED. EGNATIUS, FOL. a IXᵛ

wise that of Probus on the *Bucolics* and the *Georgics*, feeling sure, as he says, that the work will delight his noble patron both for its learning and for its novelty (Figure 116).[88] Evidently Probus's commentary had not been very widely circulated since it appeared in the

FIGURE 117. THE APPROACH TO SALÒ, LAKE GARDA

editio princeps of 1471. Of the *editio princeps* itself I have unluckily been unable, thus far, to secure a photograph.[89]

"Well, never mind. Just look out on the lake for a minute."

We were approaching the majestic cliffs by Salò, and before long steamed round into its harbor (Figure 118).

Can you keep your eyes on the scenery and open your ears to textual criticism? I asked. "Yes indeed — provided that your eyes don't miss the glorious things that pass us. What about the four witnesses — and the fifth?" Well, you will notice that all three manuscripts are late — for a fifteenth-century manuscript is late in the general history of the transmission of texts. If the Paris manuscript were, let us say, of the ninth century, the Munich of the tenth and the Vatican of the twelfth, the value of their evidence would be considerably greater. But knowing that they all are no earlier than the fifteenth century, and very possibly of the end and not the beginning of that century — that is true of Crinitus's copy, and remember that Probus's work was a novelty in 1507 — we suspect that they may have come from one and the selfsame source. In that case we may expect the three manuscripts to show certain common errors which they each derived independently from their parent manuscript. Such errors may be pointed out. One is an obvious omission in the text, which Conway with greater ingenuity and probability than any of his predecessors, has endeavored to supply.

These three witnesses, therefore, are reduced to one, the manuscript whence P, M and V were copied. There are certain indications that it itself was not particularly ancient.[90] I fancy, too, that it was written in a rather difficult hand, otherwise V would not have committed so howling an error as that of *phresgum* for *phrygium*. The text of the *editio princeps* is unhappily not at our disposal just now, but unless it should contain an altogether different text, it rather looks as though our *bataille des témoins* is one against one rather than one against four.

Of course one may suspect the credibility of Egnatius, since he is a humanistic editor. But look at his page of Probus once more (Figure 115). His source had the same omission as the other manuscripts, and he evidently was aware of the fact since he leaves part of lines 5 and 6 blank. His order of words at this point, however, differs from that in the other manuscripts, and is followed by Conway in his restoration of the text.[91]

Moreover there is one passage in which it seems to me clearer than the day that Egnatius had at his disposal a source other than the text followed by the manuscripts accessible to us. Note that he leaves a lacuna in line 9 (Figure 115). In the other manuscripts there

FIGURE 118. SALÒ

is no uncertainty here; the words *annis liberali* intervene after *pluribus*, make perfect sense and have never been suspected by editors. If Egnatius had merely followed the *editio princeps* or the source of the manuscripts M, V and P, he would have found no gap at this place. Evidently there was either a gap, or something hard to read, in the manuscript that he followed.[92] Let me draw a rough diagram to represent these family relationships.

Quick! We are coming into Gardone with its grand hotels. I suspend operations, while we think of Pietro who, with an eye to comfortable quarters and a triumphant entrance, had urged us to include Gardone in our itinerary. We glide on to Fasano with its more restful charm — to Moderno, where the sweet church bells are ringing. By this time I have drawn the following family tree.

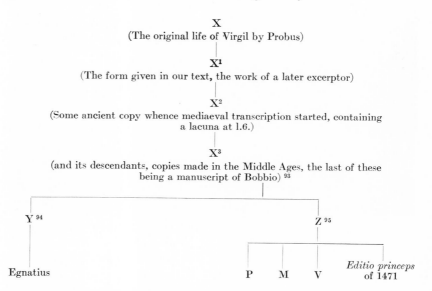

FIGURE 119. STEMMA OF THE MANUSCRIPTS OF PROBUS'S *VITA VIRGILI*

How's that? "Certainly most impressive. Anybody can see from this diagram that we should not confront Egnatius with P, M and V, and the *editio princeps*, but compare Y and Z in an attempt to get at the reading of X^2." That's it. X^3, or some descendant, represents the lost codex of Bobbio, to which Egnatius had immediate access, while P, M and V depend on some humanistic copy of it. Now, then, for the contest between three and thirty. But just a minute! Here we come to Gargnano with sail boats in its harbor and statues on its house roofs. The sails are of subtle shades of rust —

FIGURE 120. GARGNANO

ferrugineus — and there are wonderful shimmerings of light blue on the water.

It is the hour for lunch. We have brought enough with us, luckily, for the oily viands served on board are not attractive — nor the sight of one of the lunchers, applying a macaroni technique to the eating of string beans.

But Three and Thirty! They are stripped for the fight. And will the blow from the *lectio difficilior* settle the case? That principle did not work in the reading *cavisset* accepted from Egnatius by Conway. *quamuis damnat* read the three manuscripts — but did Probus use *quamuis* with the indicative? Some modern editors think so;[96] or possibly they infer that not Probus but the later compiler who extracted portions from his work is responsible for the phrase. Egnatius's conservatism is shown by his reluctance to fill in the two lacunae that he found in his source. Let us give him the credit for finding *cavisset* there, and not suspect him of a violent conjectural emendation of *damnat*. The latter is the *lectio difficilior*, but, if we follow Conway, we must suppose that it is a curious error, an attempt at a gloss, perhaps, that in the frequent fashion of glosses ousted the original *cavisset* from the text.

And so it is with *tria* and *triginta*. The latter could hardly seem a suspicious reading to a monastic scribe of the Middle Ages, or even to the corrector in his scriptorium. Their business was to reproduce what the original gave rather than to improve. Attempts at improvement, of course, may be illustrated in mediaeval manuscripts, but the art is casual, exceptional and not particularly intelligent, in comparison with the ordinary procedure of scholars of the Renaissance or modern editors, who aim to present a large circle of readers with an understandable text. While acknowledging that *tria* might be an attempt to correct *triginta* on the part of some scribe or supervisor who knew the tradition about Pietole, I find it easier to believe that — let us consult our diagram once more — the mediaeval manuscript from which Y and Z were copied (X^3 or a descendant of it) was written in a difficult hand with plenty of abbreviations, and that *tria*, written "ͭa," or the like, was understood by the copyist Z to represent *triginta*. The alteration, therefore, was nothing deliberate;

it was a mere scribal error. Y, on the other hand, might have correctly interpreted the symbol with · III ·, and Egnatius then have copied just what he found. This reasoning contains hypothetical elements, of course. But I certainly do find room for hesitation on the part of a

FIGURE 121. VILLAGE ON THE CRAGS NEAR CAMPIONE

scholar of even considerable critical experience to accept *triginta* as the undoubted reading of the text.[97]

We finish our lunch, and these other ruminations, as the boat glides along by mountains that become more and more precipitous in the narrower portion of the lake. We stop a moment at the small village of Campione — great excitement among the inhabitants as the monster vessel comes to rest at the dock. Campione is almost entirely a cotton factory village, with the standardized cottages that such an establishment necessitates — Tityrus had a better lot. Upon the heights is perched a tiny hamlet, though not too tiny to have its little church — the steeple may be seen at the right of the tallest cliff in the picture. It is one of Virgil's towns, which somebody had picked up and set on the sheer crags.[98]

"So Probus had *tria* and was right after all?" Well, I rather think he was. Let's reckon for a moment with the distance of 30 Roman miles. Let us also assume that our reasonings about the ancient boundary of the township of Mantua, based on the modern boundary, are worthy of consideration. If we lay out on the map a line representing 45 kilometres or 30 Roman miles and taking as a centre the centre of the modern town, swing this radius around the confines of the *provincia*, at no point will it fall within. Indeed, although Conway says that Calvisano is *exactly* 30 miles away,[99] this radius actually goes beyond Calvisano, if I reckon rightly, 3.6 kilometres or 2.4 Roman miles, and beyond Carpenedolo 8.5 kilometres or 5.6 miles. Ancient measurements were taken, I suppose, from the figures on milestones on a Roman road, which was not arrow-straight at all points. Such an estimate might possibly bring Calvisano to the 30 mile point, but hardly, I should think, Carpenedolo. In any case, if our suspicions about the ancient boundary are correct, both towns lay outside Mantua. If, after all, Probus, or his compiler, had *triginta*, that is wrong. Both were human and either could err. The little life of Virgil, valuable as it is, contains, at least in its present form, certain questionable statements.[100]

But a truce to Probus and his compiler — a truce of a moment at least — for our attention is wholly fixed by the grandeur of the mountains and the tossing of the waves. The shifting outlines of the precipitous heights remind us of the stupendous views that the voyager in Alaskan waters sees.

IN QUEST OF VIRGIL'S BIRTHPLACE

A fresh gale blows dead ahead. The view down the lake covers an almost oceanic stretch. We cross to the right bank and stop at Malcesine with a good beach, a fine old castle and the attractive Hotel Malcesine. Olives abound and oleanders in bloom and there is the palm, not here exotic. Now to the left bank again, to salute

FIGURE 122. CLIFFS ON LAKE GARDA

Limone, proud bearer of that name because there lemons were first grown in Europe. The gorge of the Ponale parts the mountains at that point. Through it the Italian troops made their way to the front in 1915, when their country came into the War. The end of the lake loses nothing of its magnificence: in the distance, Riva, our haven, is in sight.

"You haven't much time left." Not much — and we will take no more than the minutes allow. Please don't think I would discredit

Probus. His was one of the greatest names in Roman scholarship, and the little *Vita* of Virgil that prefaces his commentary is valuable in more ways than one. But it is obviously a mere extract made by some later compiler, who may well have bungled what he found. In any case, we should at least mention the fact that those thirty miles

FIGURE 123. APPROACH TO RIVA, ON LAKE GARDA

may be matched with a different statement in the life of the poet by Donatus. This life, as is generally agreed,[101] is based on that written by Suetonius, a contemporary of Probus and an expert biographer — not a scientific biographer in the modern sense, but one with a capacity for finding heaps of interesting things that either Truth or Rumor had reported of the subject of his sketch; he is avid for both airy legends and solid facts.[102]

In the latter category belongs the statement that the poet was born in the first consulship of Pompey the Great and Marcus Licinius Crassus on the ides of October in a village which is called Andes and which lies *not far* from Mantua.[103] Such language clearly cannot apply to Calvisano or Carpenedolo. Suetonius is locating a village of the township of Mantua with reference to the city itself. A village

FIGURE 124. RIVA FROM LAKE GARDA

near the border — allowing, for the moment, that Calvisano (Carpenedolo) is within the border — thirty miles away is not *non procul* from the centre. I am more than ever inclined to regard *triginta* as a mediaeval scribal miscopying of *tria,* and not to father upon either Probus or his compiler an error so grotesque.

Furthermore, supposing that a name like that of Probus had sanctioned the idea that Andes was 30 miles away, should we not have some echo of that tradition among later biographers or commentators? Besides the life by Suetonius-Donatus and that by Probus, some ten accounts of the poet found in other commentators are included in recent editions of *Vitae Vergilianae*.[104] All of these depend in the last resort on the life by Suetonius-Donatus. Most of these mention Andes, and it is always placed *haud procul a Mantua* or *iuxta Mantuam* or *prope Mantua*. St. Jerome, also, in his famous chronicle, has no different tradition to report.[105] Suetonius had carried all before him. Perhaps Probus, if he wrote *triginta*, is the voice of one crying in the wilderness — if so, he was not heard. I prefer to think that he would be slightly surprised, and not particularly pleased, to learn that he had located Andes thirty miles away from the mother town.

We are not so far from Riva, and soon we land. It is a picturesque place, with splendid views of the lake. Here we might rest forever. But our course takes us on to Bolzano in the heart of the Tridentine region, *Italia redenta*, wrested again from Raetians and Vindelicians, with the ancient boundaries of Augustus restored. There will be peaceful penetration and the gradual infusion of Italian feeling — a task for patience and for time, but a certain goal in prospect. For a while, a double standard and a bilingual culture, with shop signs *utriusque linguae*, — useful rosetta-stones for travellers a bit shaky in either of the two — but before many decades, the language of Dante, *piena di dolcissima ed amabilissima bellezza*.[106] We choose a little garden jutting out into the lake, with two hours or more before our train for Rovereto. Peaceful penetration has worked downwards as well as upwards. Here is a sign of *deutsche Kultur* — the dark, cool beer of Munich. "*Fass* est et ab hoste doceri," I murmur, as I bury my nose in the roomy mug. Lucky that my consort, similarly immersed, had no ears for an outrage to two languages in one pun.

[146]

"Well, the conclusion of the matter?" Why, to give it in a word, the arguments for Calvisano (Carpenedolo) we have disposed of one

FIGURE 125. AT RIVA

by one. Nor if they are united do they have the strength of *fasces*. Virgil was born in the village of Andes "not far" from Mantua, his

[147]

mother town. Probus gave the distance correctly as three miles, which a mediaeval inadvertence made thirty. Tradition had identified the village with Pietole by Dante's time, nor have we any better guide than that tradition to follow. Virgil did not stay in his birthplace long. His schooling he had mainly at Cremona, later at Milan and then at Rome. He wandered about his native district and saw with his own eyes other things than the lowland in which he was born. He began with other poetry than pastoral, schooling his imagination by reading vastly in the poets, both Greek and Roman. There is no proof whatever that he wrote his pastorals while still at Mantua — or Cremona — or Milan. It may well be that some of them were sketched on the banks of the Galaesus, down by Tarentum. The deep well of his mind — "Ah, there you go. John Lowes again." Yes, John Lowes again and again. The deep well of his mind was filled by that time with the varied splendors of Italy as well as with the varied splendors of Theocritus and others who had sung of grottoes and beech trees and the shadowy hills. From these stored impressions, whether they came from meadow, stream and grove or from no less living poetry, he fashioned, with the vivid force of his genius, a new Arcadia, touched here and there with reminiscences of the dear land of his birth, but unapproachedly transcending any part of it.

Why, then, pin the poet's fancies to the ridge of Carpenedolo, sticking up like a thumb in the middle of the plain? And why, oh why, suppose that Virgil could, or would, restrict his Arcadian imagination to one set of eclogues and his local colorings to another and then, when they were done, that he arranged them in a mechanical alternation? Virgil's mind did not operate in that way. Really, when he was at work on the *Third Eclogue*, for instance, did he say,

"See here. This is the time for Mantuan setting. Careful! Everything here must be real!" If his imagination was fettered with this iron rule, it slipped the fetters now and then; the Golden Age as well as Mantuan sluices may be found in the *Third Eclogue*, and the mixture of diversities in the *Fifth Eclogue*, the next one to be written, is, as we have seen, even more patent. It is local, why? Why, because it contains a grotto. Grottoes are Theocritean enough, but there are holes of size in the ridge of Carpenedolo. Hence the scenery is local and hence when the poet made up his little book, he gave this eclogue one of the odd numbers. I wonder if so fine a connoisseur of poetry as our friend Conway really believes all that.

I'll grant, once more, that two different elements make up the *Eclogues* and their setting; we may call them, for lack of better terms, realistic and ideal — and both are no less conspicuous in the art of Theocritus. But scenery, real or ideal, is but one aspect of a larger consideration. We also find in the *Eclogues*, besides Theocritean shepherds, real Roman persons and real Roman events. Some years ago, the noted German scholar Leo proposed to distinguish the *Eclogues*, like the comedies of early Rome, as *togatae* or *palliatae* according to the dress that they wore, the atmosphere that they reflected, Roman or Greek. Thus the *First*, the *Fourth* and the *Ninth Eclogues* may be called *togatae* — the *Fourth* most of all. But not all of the *Fourth* is purely Roman. Its scenery, by Conway's principle, is imaginary — and yet a real Roman child is born and a real Roman consul is lauded by name. Love's labor is lost when we try to affix the label "real" or "ideal" or "local" or "imaginary" or "Greek" or "Roman" to any particular poem in the *Eclogues*. Pin them all on.

And so with the allegory of contemporary events. Pastoral is the form of his poems and yet the poet sang of something real, the great injustice of the years following B.C. 43. In the confiscations of that time, his father lost, or came near losing, his farm at Andes, and the township of Mantua lost from north to south, "from where the hills melt into the plain down to the ancient beeches and the water," fifteen miles of territory measured from the boundary of Cremona and assigned to the latter town. Of the three miles remaining, the grasping Varus left the Mantuans nothing but the marshes outside the city. Some harm came to the poet himself — of that the commentators have curious things to say — but his songs availed something even if the greater loss persisted for a time. That much we see in the *Eclogues* — it is one theme among many — suggested, not described in detailed preciseness. It is a bit of local history, that, like the bits of personal history and the bits of Mantuan landscape, is caught up by the poet, transmuted by his imagination and made part of his audacious but harmonious plan. Such "incongruities" never will trouble simple and poetic readers of the *Eclogues*, who, whatever may be the meaning, surrender to the charm. Not that we should not try to get that meaning. The more we search, the more we find, confessing, however, an ultimate defeat, like gaping rustics spellbound by the magician's art. But now, let's talk about something else.

The bar-maid, arms akimbo, was watching us from the door-way.

"Signorina — Fräulein — ancora due — noch zwei dunkele, bitte schön."

VIRGIL AT PIETOLE

NOTES

NOTES

1 (3). *Purgatorio*, XVIII, 82.

2 (3). In particular Suetonius, whose life of Virgil is preserved in an enlarged form in the commentary written by Donatus in the fourth century.

3 (3). *Georgics*, I, 412: "nescio qua praeter solitum dulcedine laeti."

4 (4). *Aen.*, VII, 3: "Et nunc servat honos sedem tuus."

5 (4). *Georgics*, III, 10:

> primus ego in patriam mecum, modo vita supersit,
> Aonio rediens deducam vertice Musas;
> primus Idumaeas referam tibi, Mantua, palmas,
> et viridi in campo templum de marmore ponam
> propter aquam, tardis ingens ubi flexibus errat
> Mincius et tenera praetexit harundine ripas.

6 (4). R. S. Conway, "Where was Virgil's Farm?" being Chapter II of his *Harvard Lectures on the Vergilian Age*, Cambridge, Harvard University Press, 1928. Professor Conway had first presented his views on the subject in a lecture given at the John Rylands Library of Manchester in 1923. He gives to his former colleague, Professor G. E. K. Braunholtz, the credit for the initial suggestion, or "discovery," made in 1915. See pp. 14 f.

7 (4). *Vitae Vergilianae*, recensuit Iacobus Brummer, Leipzig, 1912, p. 73, 1: "P. Vergilius Maro natus Idibus Octobris Crasso et Pompeio consulibus matre Magia Polla, patre Vergilio rustico vico Andico, qui abest a Mantua milia passuum XXX."

8 (5). See Conway, *op. cit.*, p. 19.

9 (6). *Ecl.*, ix, 7:

> Certe equidem audieram, qua se subducere colles
> incipiunt mollique iugum demittere clivo,
> usque ad aquam et veteres, iam fracta cacumina, fagos,
> omnia carminibus vestrum servasse Menalcan.

NOTES

10 (6). Conway, *op. cit.*, p. 31.

11 (7). Donatus, *Vita Vergili*, ed. Brummer, *op. cit.*, p. 2, 20: "initia aetatis Cremonae egit usque ad virilem togam, quam XV anno natali suo accepit isdem illis consulibus iterum [duobus], quibus erat natus."

12 (7). *Ibid.*, p. 2, 11: "cum marito rus propinquum petens ex itinere divertit atque in subiecta fossa partu levata est."

13 (11). See the restoration of the "House of Diana" by I. Gisimondi, Fig. 20 (p. 65) in G. Calza, *Ostia, Historical Guide to the Monuments* (translated by R. Weeden-Cooke), Milan-Rome, 1925. I am indebted to Professor Calza (and to Director Stevens of the American Academy in Rome) for the photograph here reproduced. The house was merely a tenement. For a reproduction of a palace, see Calza's article in *Art and Archaeology*, XII (1921), 215.

14 (15). *Rerum Rusticarum Lib.*, I, vii, 10: "Caesar Vopiscus aedilicius causam cum ageret apud censores, campos Roseae Italiae dixit esse sumen in quo relicta pertica postridie non appareret propter herbam."

15 (15). *Georgics*, II, 198:
et qualem infelix amisit Mantua campum
pascentem niveos herboso flumine cycnos;
non liquidi gregibus fontes, non gramina deerunt,
et quantum longis carpent armenta diebus
exigua tantum gelidus ros nocte reponet.

16 (15). *Georgics*, IV, 425:
iam rapidus torrens sitientis Sirius Indos
ardebat caelo, et medium sol igneus orbem
hauserat; arebant herbae, et cava flumina siccis
faucibus ad limum radii tepefacta coquebant.

17 (16). *Georgics*, I, 79:
arida tantum
ne saturare fimo pingui pudeat sola neve
effetos cinerem immundum iactare per agros.

NOTES

18 (18). *Georgics*, II, 434:

> quid maiora sequar? salices humilesque genistae,
> aut illae pecori frondem aut pastoribus umbram
> sufficiunt saepemque satis et pabula melli.

19 (19). John Sargeaunt, *The Trees, Shrubs and Plants of Virgil*, Oxford, 1920, p. 49.

20 (19). The author of the *Brevis Expositio Vergilii Georgicorum* (*Servii Grammatici qui feruntur in Vergilii Carmina Commentarii*, ed. Thilo and Hagen, Leipzig, III, 2 [1902], p. 311) sees a difficulty but solves it in the wrong way. He explains *humiles* as *infructuosae* and asks: "Nam quemadmodum sunt humiles, si umbras pastoribus faciunt?" Let us give *humiles* its natural sense of 'lowly,' here 'low-growing,' 'near to the ground (*humus*),' and find its appropriateness in what I have endeavored to set forth.

21 (19). *Ecl.*, III, 111:

> claudite iam rivos, pueri; sat prata biberunt.

22 (21). *Georgics*, IV, 121:

> tortusque per herbam
> cresceret in ventrem cucumis.

23 (21). If *tortus* refers to the shape of the melon, it may be the *cocomero serpentino* as Tenore supposes. See Conington on the passage (after Keightley). I agree, however, with those, like Conington, who understand *tortus* to describe the vine's meandering through the grass.

24 (21). See L. H. Bailey, *Cyclopaedia of American Horticulture*, New York, VI, (1906) 1967.

25 (21). Quoted in the *Encyclopaedia Britannica*, 11th edition (1911), XVIII, 98. The most recent discussion is that of R. Billiard, in *L'Agriculture dans l'Antiquité d'après les Géorgiques de Virgile* (Paris, Boccard, 1928), p. 477. He inclines to believe, on grounds that appear to me inconclusive, that the melon came to Italy somewhat after Virgil's time.

NOTES

26 (28). *Georgics*, IV, 271:

> est etiam flos in pratis cui nomen amello
> fecere agricolae, facilis quaerentibus herba;
> namque uno ingentem tollit de caespite silvam
> aureus ipse, sed in foliis, quae plurima circum
> funduntur, violae sublucet purpura nigrae;
> saepe deum nexis ornatae torquibus arae;
> asper in ore sapor; tonsis in vallibus illum
> pastores et curva legunt prope flumina Mellae.

27 (35). *Op. cit.*, p. 31, Plates 8 and 9.

28 (35). *Georgics*, II, 388:

> et te, Bacche, vocant per carmina laeta, tibique
> oscilla ex alta suspendunt mollia pinu.
> hinc omnis largo pubescit vinea fetu,
> complentur vallesque cavae saltusque profundi
> et quocumque deus circum caput egit honestum.

29 (39). Horace, *Satires*, I, 5, 48:

> Lusum it Maecenas, dormitum ego Vergiliusque;
> namque pila lippis inimicum et ludere crudis.

30 (41). *Op. cit.*, p. 29, Plate 3.

31 (48). *Op. cit.*, p. 29, Plate 4.

32 (56). *Georgics*, II, 146:

> hinc albi, Clitumne, greges et maxima taurus
> victima, saepe tuo perfusi flumine sacro,
> Romanos ad templa deum duxere triumphos.

33 (57). On the Gonzaga family, see Selwyn Brinton, *The Gonzaga, Lords of Mantua*, London, 1927. On *La Virgiliana*, see Restori, *Mantova e dintorni*, Mantua, 1915, p. 432. I am indebted for the latter reference, and for various other bits of information, to Professor Nardi.

34 (58). *Epodes*, II, 9:

> adulta vitium propagine
> altas maritat populos.

NOTES

35 (61). *Idylls*, VII, 10:

κοὔπω τὰν μεσάταν ὁδὸν ἄνυμες, οὐδὲ τὸ σᾶμω / ἁμὶν τὸ Βρασίλα κατεφαίνετο.

36 (61). *Aen.*, X, 199. He there is called Ocnus, as Servius notes on the present passage.

37 (61). Signor Balzo of Mantua, quoted by Professor Conway on p. 22, n. 2, has scored a good point in his reference to this monument. Professor Conway rather inclines to demolish the tomb of Bianor, or, allowing for its existence, to show that Signor Balzo has reckoned without trigonometry. But has he not himself reckoned without optics or the nature of a country road? Even supposing a mathematically straight and unencumbered road and shepherds with Lyncean eyes, we still must explain the disinclination of Moeris to be eased of the kids he is carrying when the two had fifteen more miles to go.

38 (61). It is no part of my programme to identify the scenery of the *Eclogues* too closely with what may be seen near Mantua, but I cannot help observing that the much discussed *aequor* (v. 37) is by no means an inapt term for the Mantuan lagoon as seen by wayfarers approaching the town. See Figure 31. But here I would abide by Servius (Donatus) who explains the word as *spatium campi* (Thilo and Hagen, *op. cit.*, III, 1, p. 117). We may note incidentally, however, that Servius in *Ecl.*, I, 48 (*Ibid.*, p. 11) notes: PALVS id est aequor.

39 (61). I learn from Professor Nardi that the fort, constructed in the time of Napoleon I, is known neither as S. Virgilio nor S. Vigilio, but simply as the Forte di Pietole. Possibly Pietro was repeating a barrack-room invention. The construction of the fort meant the destruction of the ancient Pietole. See above, p. 51.

40 (69). See above, p. 5.

41 (70). P. 32, Plate 7.

42 (70). P. 30, Plate 5.

43 (74). See G. H. Hallam, *Horace at Tibur and the Sabine Farm*, sec. ed., Harrow, 1927.

44 (74). See Conway, p. 27, n. 4.

NOTES

45 (75). See above, p. 6, n. 9.

46 (75). The measurements given in this book are taken from the excellent map published by the Istituto Geografico Militare, 1924, to which I will refer as the Military Map. In this case, I take the shortest distance from the centre of the town to the river. In one instance, more than one map are used; see below, p. 142, n. 99.

47 (76). *Eclogues*, I, 46:

> Fortunate senex, ergo tua rura manebunt
> et tibi magna satis, quamvis lapis omnia nudus
> limosoque palus obducat pascua iunco;
> non insueta gravis temptabunt pabula fetas,
> nec mala vicini pecoris contagia laedent.
> fortunate senex, hic inter flumina nota
> et fontis sacros frigus captabis opacum.
> hinc tibi quae semper vicino ab limite saepes
> Hyblaeis apibus florem depasta salicti
> saepe levi somnum suadebit inire susurro.
> hinc alta sub rupe canet frondator ad auras
> nec tamen interea raucae, tua cura, palumbes,
> nec gemere aëria cessabit turtur ab ulmo.

Incidentally, if Tityrus stands for Virgil, why is our youthful poet called *senex*? Servius comes bravely to the rescue (Thilo and Hagen, *op. cit.*, p. 11): FORTUNATE SENEX non ad aetatem Vergilii refert, sed ad fortunam futuram, praesago usus verbo. We should translate, therefore, "Happy young man, destined to reach a ripe old age undisturbed on your pleasant little farm!" (!) But Tityrus has obviously been a slave, now freed by the young god at Rome, and he has had a succession of mistresses. This, too, makes curious autobiography for Virgil. The whole is a fable for searchers after allegory in the *Eclogues*. See above, p. 79.

48 (76). Is Conway right, then (p. 27), in calling Meliboeus a "near neighbor" of Tityrus?

NOTES

49 (78). Conway, perforce (p. 27), makes the shepherds live "near some small town." I prefer Servius (Thilo and Hagen, *op. cit.*, p. 8) on l. 20: NOSTRAE autem Mantuae.

50 (78). Conway (p. 31) notes the distance from Calvisano as 8½ English miles. But why bring in Calvisano when the farm has been definitely located at Carpenedolo?

51 (78). It is *hic* (not *illic*) *inter flumina nota*.

52 (78). Servius (*op. cit.*, p. 12) on l. 51: "INTER FLUMINA Padum et Mincium." I hardly think, however, that we need to go down so far as the Po.

53 (79). See above, p. 76, n. 47. Excellent remarks on Virgil's art will be found in Nardi, *op. cit.*, p. 115 f.

54 (83). Through the kind intercession of my colleague Professor J. D. M. Ford, Professor H. H. Vaughan of the University of California informs me that the phrase *Al cantù el vì l'è bù* is good Brescian and that in Mantua one would say *Al canton 'l vin l'è bon.*

55 (84). Mommsen discusses the inscriptions from the *Ager Mantuanus* in C. I. L. V, 406, but draws no certain conclusions as to the ancient limits of the township. Conway notes (p. 22) that in 1797 Castiglione and Asola belonged to Brescia. It were better for his argument if he could point to villages now in the provincia of Brescia that once were reckoned as Mantuan.

56 (84). So Conway (p. 20), but see above, p. 142.

57 (84). See Conway (pp. 32, 38, Plate 12). In the gray sky that hung over Calvisano as we passed through we could not see the mountains at all.

58 (95). *Ibid.*, p. 19. From the Index to the *Corpus Inscriptionum Latinarum*, V, s. v. *Vergilius*, I can find only six inscriptions extant today that bear the names *Vergilius* or *Vergilia* (1283, 1446, 3828, 4137, 6785, 7567). The two inscriptions under 3827 are copies of originals now lost. Very possibly my hasty search was imperfect. It is clear in any case that the number of Virgilian inscriptions is scanty.

NOTES

59 (96). See the Index to C. I. L. V. s. v. *Magius, Magia.*

60 (96). Brummer. *Vitae Vergilianae*, p. 1, 2: "patre, quem quidam opificem figulum, plures Magi cuiusdam viatoris initio mercennarum, mox ob industriam generum tradiderunt."

61 (96). I am indebted to Professor Alessandro Scrinsi, director of the Museum at Brescia for securing for me the excellent photographs here reproduced. On the meaning of the inscriptions see Conway's admirable treatment, pp. 19–22, 39–40.

62 (98). Pp. 21–22. At the top of p. 21 the statement is not quite so precise: "probably, if not certainly, in the first century of the Empire."

63 (100). On the *I longa*, see R. Cagnat, *Cours d'Épigraphie Latine*, 4me édition, Paris, 1914, p. 17. Introduced in the time of Sulla to denote the diphthong EI, it later became merely "une habitude graphique." So it is, for instance, in the famous inscription of the Arval Brethren of 59 A.D. (E. Diehl, *Inscriptiones Latinae*, Bonn, 1912, Plate 25) and so it is in the present inscription, which I feel belongs in about the same period. In the later centuries, *I longa* tends to disappear in inscriptions. After writing this note, I sent the photographs of the inscriptions to my friend Professor James C. Egbert, author of the well-known and useful work, "Introduction to the Study of Latin Inscriptions" (New York, 1895), who replied, "I am inclined to date the P. MAGIUS inscription in the third quarter of the first century after Christ. The VERGILIA inscription belongs in about the same period or somewhat later."

64 (103). *Gesta Friderici I. Imperatoris* (ed. alt., recens. G. Waitz, *Scriptores Rerum Germanicarum in usum scholarum*, Hannover, 1884), II, 29 (21): "Revertantur, opto, pristina tempora; redeant, rogo, inclitae Urbis privilegia . . . Assurexi tuae ac divae rei publicae profuturum gloriae, ad sacrum sanctae Urbis senatum equestremque ordinem instaurandum.

NOTES

65 (103). *Ibid.*, I, 29 (28):

> Rex valeat, quidquid cupit optineat super hostes,
> Imperium teneat, Romae sedeat, regat orbem
> Princeps terrarum, ceu fecit Iustinianus.
> Cesaris accipiat cesar quae sunt sua presul,
> Ut Christus iussit, Petro solvente tributum.

This is from a letter sent by the Romans to Conrad, the predecessor of Frederick, in 1149. What GT stands for, if I copied it correctly, I do not know. One would expect EPL or EP.

66 (104). See Mommsen's note on C. I. L. V 3827 (b).

67 (104). Pp. 23–25, with Anderson's note, p. 23.

68 (104). On his services to Aldus in connection with the ancient *codex Parisinus* of Pliny's *Letters*, see *e. g.*, E. G. Hardy, *C. Plinii Caecilii Secundi Epistulae ad Traianum Imperatorem cum eiusdem Responsis*, London, 1889, pp. 67 ff.

69 (105). P. 23. Nardi has shown (*op. cit.*, p. 105–109) that Virgilian legends clustered about Pietole long before Dante's time.

70 (107). P. 31, n. 3.

71 (112). Middleton and Mills, *Student's Companion to Latin Authors*, London, 1896, p. 148. This passage was brought to Professor Conway's attention by Professor Anderson. A similar view was held in the eighteenth century by one of the greatest of Italian scholars, Scipione Maffei. See Nardi, *op. cit.*, p. 110.

72 (112) Pp. 38 f.

73 (113). Servius on *Ecl.*, IX, 10 (Thilo and Hagen, *op. cit.*, III, 1, p. 110): "CARMINIBVS VESTRVM SERVASSE MENALCAN id est vestrum Vergilium *cuius causa agri Mantuanis redditi sunt.*"

74 (113). On *Ecl.*, IX, 7 (*ibid.*, p. 109): "SVBDVCERE . . . *usque ad eum autem locum perticam limitarem Octavius Musa porrexerat, limitator ab Augusto datus, id est per quindecim milia passuum agri Mantuani, cum Cremonensis non sufficeret, offensus a Mantuanis, quod pecora eius in agro publico aliquando clausissent.*"

NOTES

75 (114). On *Ecl.*, IX, 10 (*ibid.*, p. 110): "OMNIA quae supra dixit, intellegamus autem, aut Vergilii tantum agrum, aut totius Mantuae esse descriptum, *quod alii dicunt Vergilium ostendere voluisse, quod Mantuanis per iniquitatem Alfeni Vari, qui agros divisit, praeter palustria nihil relictum sit. sicut ex oratione Cornelii in Alfenum ostenditur, 'cum iussus tria milia passus a muro in diversa relinquere, vix octingentos passus aquae, quae circumdata est, admetireris, reliquisti.'*"

76 (114). See Map No. 3.

77 (115). *Georgics*, II, 198–202. See above, p. 15, n. 15.

78 (116). I had come to this conclusion before reading Nardi and G. Funaioli (reviewing Hubaux, *Le réalisme de Virgile*) in *Aevum*, II (1928), 433 f. The latter rightly calls attention to the emphasis on *omnia*, which "sembra significare qualcosa più che un pezzo di terra, proprietà d'un solo." Nardi also makes it possible to believe that there was once an actual *mons Virgilii* near Pietole itself, so that the poet's description, after all, might have applied to an estate at Pietole. See *op. cit.*, pp. 113–115.

79 (116). I thoroughly agree with that part of the note contributed by Anderson to Conway's essay (p. 39) in which he concludes that "Mantua must have lost a considerable stretch of territory to the north."

80 (123). P. 36.

81 (123). Nardi deserves the credit for calling attention to this edition (*op. cit.*, p. 103).

82 (123). See his edition, quire P p.[vi^v] (in the Harvard copy, p. 174^v): "In Bucolicis quod ad Probi commentariolum attinet secuti sumus vetustatem illam quemadmodum ex vetustissimo codice manu scripto Bobii quondam a Georgio Merula inuento adnotauimus." The year of the discovery was apparently 1493; see Thilo and Hagen, *op. cit.*, III, 2, p. viii. It has recently been suspected that the commentary of Probus was known before 1493; see *e. g.*, P. Wessner, *Jahresbericht*

über die Fortschritte der klassischen Altertumswissenschaft 139 (1908),
152. And now, thanks to Nardi, the evidence of the edition of 1471 is
to be added.

83 (124). I have tried to show that in the case of Aldus's praise of his ancient manuscript of Pliny the laugh is on those who belittle his statements. See "A New Approach to the Text of Pliny's Letters," I, *Harvard Studies in Classical Philology*, XXXIV (1923) 79–191, especially
80–99, 137–153, 189–191. The remarks on "Notions of palaeography
in the Renaissance" contain a more favorable estimate of the humanists than is generally made.

84 (124). P. 36.

85 (126). *Georgics*, II, 160.

86 (128). I would here express my gratitude to M. Omont of the Bibliothèque Nationale, Professor Leidinger of the Bayerische Staatsbiblio-
thek at Munich and to Monsignori Tisserant and Mercati of the Vatican Library for kindly procuring the necessary photographs for me.
Those of the edition of Egnatius come from Munich; there is also a
copy in the Harvard College Library. In the facsimiles here shown,
the size of the pages has been somewhat reduced.

87 (129). See Mommsen, *Rheinisches Museum*, XVI (1861), 138. He prints
the subscription of the humanist: *Excerpsi hactenus ego Pet: Crinitus
pridie Nonas Octobres 1496 Florentie in edibus . . . Ing (?) ad Valerium
Probum, quem mox sum integrum perscripturus, cum licebit exemplar
aliquod conveniens in opus id invenire.* He evidently expected at some
time to come across a manuscript containing the commentary to all the
rest of Virgil. Mommsen characterizes the nature of the copy with his
customary penetration: "Die Schrift ist schwer zu lesen, aber die
Abschrift an sich gut und von Emendationen oder Interpolationen
wenig oder nichts zu bemerken." See further on the Bobbio manuscript
R. Sabbadini, *Le Scoperte dei codici latini e greci nei secoli XIV e XV*,
Florence, I (1905), 132, 151.

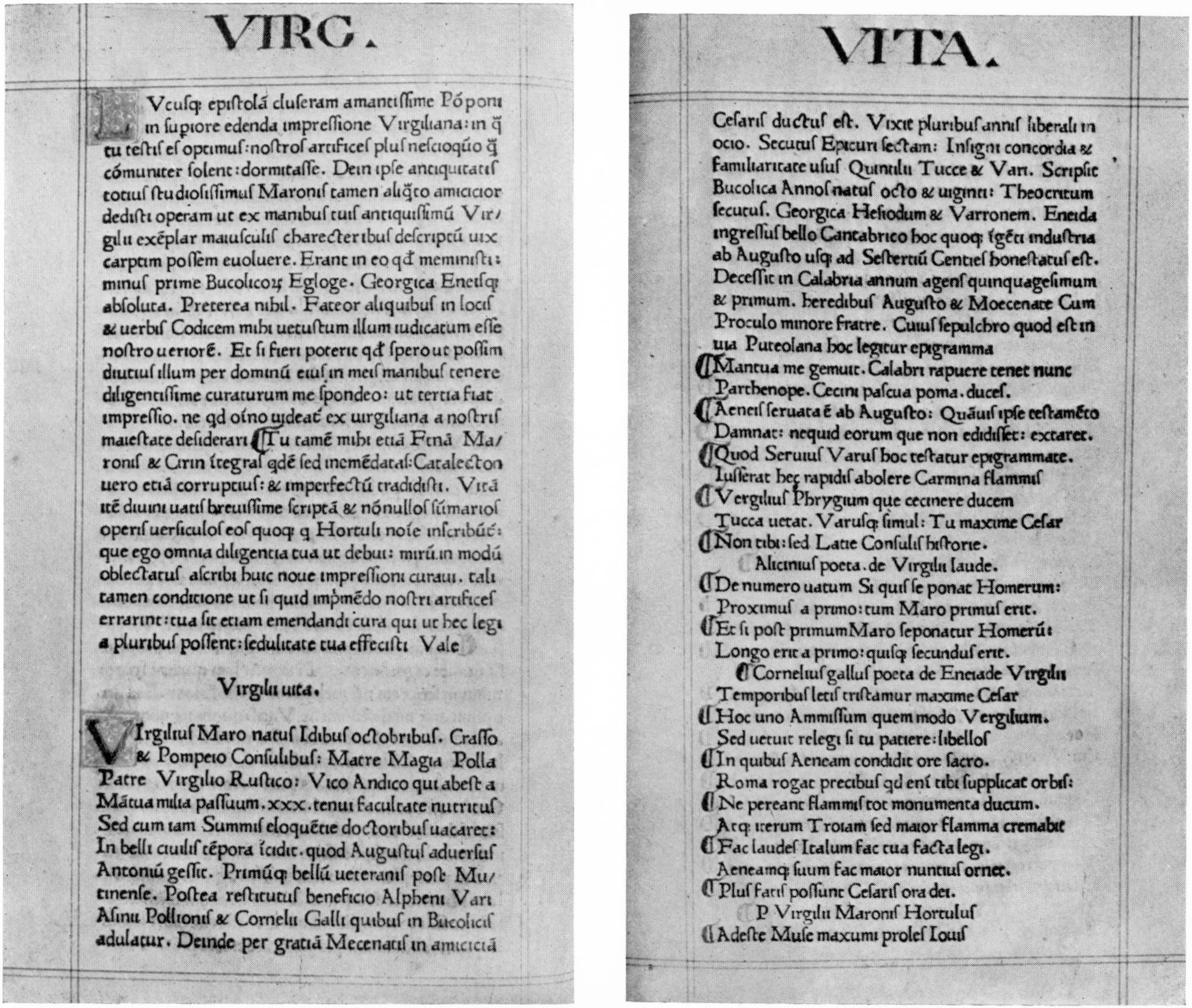

VIRG.

Vculæq epiſtolã cluſeram amantiſſime Põponi in ſupiore edenda impreſſione Virgiliana: in q̃ tu teſtis eſ optimuſ: noſtros artifices plus neſciопĩᵒ q̃ cõmunter ſolent: dormitaſſe. Dein ipſe ancquitateſ totius ſtudioſiſſimus Maronis tamen aliqᵗᵒ amicatior dediſti operam ut ex manibus tuis antiquiſſimã Vir/ gilii exẽplar mauiſcalis charecteribus deſcriptã uix carptim poſſem euoluere. Erant in eo q̃ meminiſti: minus prime Bucolicoᵣ Egloge. Georgica Eneiſq̃ abſoluta. Preterea nihil. Factor aliquibus in locis & uerbis Codicem mihi uetuſtum illum iudicatum eſſe noſtro uerrorẽ. Et ſi fieri poterit q̃ſperout poſſim ducruſ illum per domnũ eius in meis manibus tenere diligentiſſime curaturum me ſpondeo: ut tertia fiat impreſſio. ne qd oĩno uideaˀ ex uirgiliana a noſtris maeſtate deſiderari⟨Tu camẽ mihi etã Fenã Ma/ ronis & Cirin ſtegral qdẽ ſed inemẽdatã: Catalecton uero etã corruptius & imperfectũ tradidiſti. Vitã utẽ diuinã uatis fareuiſſime ſcriptã & nõnullis ſĩmarios operis uerſiculos eos quoq̃ q̃ Hortculi noĩe inſcribũˀ: que ego omnia diligentia tua ut debui: miru̇.in modũ oblectatus aſcribi huic noxie impreſſioni curaui. tali tamen condicione ut ſi quid impẽdio noſtri artifices errarint: tua ſic etiam emendandi cura qui ut hec legi a pluribus poſſint: ſeduliate tua efficiſti Vale⟩

Virgilii uita.

Virgilius Maro natus Idibus octobribus. Craſſo & Pompeo Conſulibus: Matre Maga Polla Patre Virgilio Ruſtico: Vico Andico qui abeſt a Mátua milia paſſium. xxx. tenui facultate nutritur̃ Sed cum tam Summi eloquẽtie doctoribus uacaret: In belli ciuilis tẽpora ſcit: quod Auguſtus aduerſus Antonũ geſſit. Primũq̃ belliſ ueteranis poſt Mu/ tinenſe. Poſtea refutatuſ beneficio Alpheni Varr Aſinii Pollionis & Cornelii Galli quibus in Bucolicã adulatur. Deinde per gratiã Mecenatis in amicitiã

VITA.

Ceſaris ductus eſt. Vixit pluribus annis liberalis in oco. Secutus Epicuri ſectam: Inſigni concordia & familiaritate uſus Quintilii Tucce & Varri. Scripſit Bucolica Annis natus octo & uiginti: Theocritum ſecutus. Georgica Heſiodum & Varronem. Eneida ingreſſus bello Canabrico hoc quoq̃ ſ̃gẽti induſtria ab Auguſto uſq̃ ad Seſteriũ Centeũ boneſtatus eſt. Deceſſit in Calabria annum agens quinquageſimum & primum. heredibus Auguſto & Moecenate Cum Proculo minore fratre. Cuius ſepulchro quod eſt in uia Puteolana hoc legitur epigramma

⟨Mantua me gemuit: Calabri rapuere tenet nunc Parthenope: Cecini paſcua poma. duces.

⟨Aeneis ſeruata eſt ab Auguſto: Quiſuis ipſe teſtamẽto Damnat: nequid eorum que non edidiſſet: extaret.

⟨Quod Seruius Varus hoc teſtatur epigrammate. Luſſerat hec rapidã abolere Carmina flammã

⟨Virgilius Phrygium que cecnere ducem Tucca uetat. Varuſq̃ ſimul: Tu maxime Ceſar

⟨Non obis: ſed Latie Conſulit hiſtorie.

⟨Alcimus poeta. de Virgilii laude.

⟨De numero uatum Si quis ſe ponat Homerum: Proximuſ a primo: tum Maro primus erit.

⟨Et ſi poſt primumMaro ſeponatur Homeriſ Longo errit a primo: quiſq̃ ſecundus erit.

⟨Cornelius gallus poeta de Eneaide Virgilii Temporibus latis treſtamur maxime Ceſar

⟨Hoc uno Ammiſſum quem modo Vergilium. Sed uetuit relegi ſi tu patere: libelloſ

⟨In quibus Aeneam condidit ore ſacro. Roma rogat precibus qd erit tibi ſupplicat orbis:

⟨Ne pereant flammã: tot monumenta ducum.

⟨Atq̃ rerum Troiam hel maior flamma cremabit

⟨Fac laudeſ Italum fac tua facta legi. Aeneaq̃ ſuum fac maior nuntius ornet:

⟨Plus fariſ poſſiuncent Ceſaris ora dei.

⟨P Virgilii Maronis Horrulus

⟨Adeſte Mu̇ic maxcum proles Iouis

FIGURE 126. VIRGIL, OPERA, ED. ROME, 1471
(From the copy in the Lenox... Library, Elmer...)

NOTES

88 (135). "His Probi commentariolus in Bucolica et Georgica tametsi de-
curtatus et ipse nec satis integer accedet. Cuius tibi lectio non parum
voluptatis (ut spero) nouitate sua et utilitatis eruditione allatura sit."

89 (135). I can now express my indebtedness to my friend Luigi Schia-
parelli for procuring me a photograph of the pages of Probus in the
copy of this rare edition in the Laurentian Library. There is no doubt
that its text is of the sort represented by P, M and V, though it
hardly seems, as Nardi suggested (*op. cit.*, p. 103), to be a copy of V.
See Figure 127.

90 (136). All three copies agree in the late mediaeval or Renaissance spell-
ings *buccolica* and *ocio* (Brummer, p. 73, 10). Of course all three
scribes might themselves so have spelled, but it is worthy of note that
Crinitus, who, as Mommsen (*loc. cit.*) well says, was making a careful
copy, writes *ocio* in the text but in the margin (Figure 114, l. 4) jots
down, as a phrase worth remembering, *otium liberale*. All three copies
also have the decidedly Renaissance or late mediaeval abbreviation
max^e for *maxime* at the end of a verse of poetry (Brummer, p. 74, 27).
In V, lack of space might have forced the abbreviation (though
maxime could have been closely written in) but in the other two manuscripts there is plenty of space. See Figure 114 for Crinitus (four lines
from the end), who has oceans of space. Once more, he seems to be
copying just what he found in his original — a late mediaeval or Renaissance copy, I should say, of the old Bobbio codex.

91 (137). The MSS have *primumque bellum veteranis post Mutinense postea*,
but Egnatius *primumque post Mutinense bellum veteranis postea*. Conway's method (p. 36) of supplying the gap proceeds on the plausible
hypothesis of an omission due to *homoioteleuta* (here the two-fold occur-
rence of the word *bellum*). Various other attempts to reconstruct the
omitted words start with Egnatius's text.

Conway also reads with Egnatius *cavisset* (Brummer, *op. cit.*, p. 74,
23) against *damnat* of the manuscripts. The latter also have *Varusque*
(Brummer, p. 74, 27) against Egnatius, who has the correct *Variusque*.

NOTES

See also the following note. A slight examination of the text of the commentary following the life (in Thilo and Hagen's edition) reveals at once a number of other certain instances; these need a careful study.

92 (137). Nardi, I now find, had noticed the importance of these *lacunae* (*op. cit.*, p. 104). Another instructive instance of E's independence of M P V is furnished by the very last line of the *Vita* (Brummer, p. 74, 28): *non tibi, sed Latiae consulis historiae*. This is the reading of M P V, but it really does not make sense. "You, mightiest Caesar, in saving the *Aeneid* from the flames, have a care not for yourself but for Latin history." But would it have been for the interest of Augustus to burn the poem? Was he nobly self-sacrificing in saving it? Egnatius reads *non sinis sed* — "You allow it not" — *non sinis* says the same thing as *vetat*, applied to Tucca and Varius. However, *non sinis sed* offends the metre. The solution is given by the reading in the *Vita* by Donatus, who also quotes these lines with two more besides. It is (Brummer, p. 9, 146): *non sinis et Latiae consulis historiae*. The Bobbio MS, I take it, read, by an easy dittography, *non sinis set*. Egnatius corrected this (perhaps unconsciously) to *non sinis sed*; had Egnatius proceeded in the "Humanistic" fashion, he would not have left the line thus glaringly unmetrical (and perhaps his original already had the change to *sed*). Another copy of the Bobbio MS indulged in an haplography, resulting in the unintelligible *non sini set* (or *sed*). The next copyist "improved" this to *non sibi sed*, which received a final "improvement" in the parent MS of M P and V, namely *non tibi sed*.

93 (138). This contained, of course, certain errors, *e. g.*, the gap at p. 73, 6 (Brummer) and *non sinis set* (see the preceding note).

94 (138). Among its errors are the second lacuna (Brummer, p. 73, 10) and *non sinis set* (*sed*).

95 (138). As indicated in N. 92 (p. 137), two or more copies may have intervened (Z^1, Z^2 etc.) between Z and the original of M P V. This latter MS had as errors *e. g.*, the dislocation of words at the lacuna at l. 5,

damnat for *cavisset* (l. 23) and *non tibi sed* (l. 28). It may be that P and M come from one copy of this manuscript and V from another. There are also traces of learned emendation in V. It may be that not the Bobbio MS but some other was the parent of P, M, V and the *editio princeps*. These are, for our present purpose, minor matters, which cannot be settled without an elaborate study of the text of the entire commentary.

96 (140). *E. g.*, Hagen and Brummer.

97 (141). Let me mention merely Funaioli, a textual critic of long experience and illustrious achievement, who declares that the reading *tria* is "paleograficamente di leggieri confondibile con *triginta*." (*Loc. cit.*, *Aevum*, II (1928), 434. So Nardi, no mean authority, *op. cit.*, p. 104. He also cites a Cologne edition (copied from Egnatius, apparently) for the reading III instead of XXX.

98 (142). *Georgics*, II, 156: "tot congesta manu praeruptis oppida saxis."

99 (142). I may have some error in my figures, though they represent the average of several measurements made from several maps by myself and a very careful measurer, Mr. B. M. Peebles of the Harvard Graduate School. Professor Nardi now informs me that Calvisano *is* 45 km. distant from Mantua, as the crow flies, thus supporting Conway. The distance by road (*via corrazzabile*) is about 50 km. Carpenedolo, he states, is 40 km. in a straight line, and 45 km. by road. My main point is that a radius of 30 Roman miles from Mantua would fall outside the limits of the township if the ancient boundary approximately corresponded to the modern one.

100 (142). For a recent estimate of the life and the commentary of Pseudo-Probus (for such we must call him) by a most competent authority on the Latin grammarians and commentators in general, see P. Wessner in *Jahresbericht über die Fortschritte der klassischen Altertumswissenschaft*, 139 (1908), 152. A telling point brought out by Funaioli is that the reviser of Probus *has directly copied Suetonius*. See *op. cit.*, *Aevum*,

NOTES

II (1928), 434 and *Rivista di filologia classica*, XLVIII (1920), pp. 224 f.

101 (144). The most careful demonstration of this fact is contained in the unpublished doctor's thesis (Harvard) of R. M. Geer, *Quatenus vita Vergiliana Aelio Donato attributa re vera Suetonio Tranquillo debeatur*, an outline of which is given in *Harvard Studies in Classical Philology*, XXXVII (1926), 99–100. See also his "Non-Suetonian Passages in the *Life of Vergil* formerly ascribed to Donatus," *Transactions of the American Philological Association*, LVII (1926), 107–116. He goes too far, in my opinion, in pronouncing the passage on the Minor Poems not Suetonian (p. 110).

102 (144). The most thorough account of Suetonius is that by Funaioli in Pauly-Wissowa, *Realenzyklopädie der klassischen Altertumswissenschaft*, s. v. *Suetonius*.

103 (145). Brummer, I, 5: "natus est Cn. Pompeio Magno M. Licinio Crasso primum coss. iduum Octobrium die in pago qui Andes dicitur et abest a Mantua non procul."

104 (146). Besides Brummer, that of E. Diehl, *Die Vitae Vergilianae und ihre antiken Quellen*, Bonn, 1911.

105 (146). *Eusebi Chronicorum Libri Duo*, ed. A. Schoene, Berlin, II (1866), 135: "Vergilius Maro in pago qui Andes dicitur haut procul a Mantua nascitur Pompeio et Crasso consulibus."

106 (146). *Convivio*, I, 10.

MAP 3.